awakening

awakening to the call of God

TERRY B. WALLING
w/ Zack Curry & Kyle Walling

© 2014 Terry Walling

Leader Breakthru
Resourcing and coaching breakthrough in the lives
of risk-taking, Kingdom leaders.

www.leaderbreakthru.com

Unless otherwise noted, all biblical quotations come from THE HOLY BIBLE, NEW INTERNATIONAL VERSION®, NIV® Copyright © 1973, 1978, 1984, 2011 by Biblica, Inc.® Used by permission. All rights reserved worldwide.

It takes heroic humility to be yourself, and to be nobody but the person and the artist that God intended for you to be.

—THOMAS MERTON

contents

Before Words 6
Introduction 9

1   INVITATION
    A Narrative 18
    Untangling 24

2   ENTRY
    Something More 30
    Something Else 31
    The Back Story: *Direction* 34
    Journal 39

3   EVALUATION AND ALIGNMENT
    Narrative: *The Call to See* 44
    Narrative: *The Call to Obey* 46
    The Back Story: *Identity* 48
    Journal 53

4   DIRECTION
    Threshold 60
    Destiny Revelation 62
    The Back Story: *Calling* 65
    Journal 69

5	CHALLENGE	
	Decision	74
	Faith	77
	The Back Story: *Two Tracks*	79
	Summary of the Awakening Transition	82
	Journal	87
6	POSTURES: Ways to Respond | *Kyle Walling*	
	Listening	94
	Chronicling	96
	Leaning	98
7	TRAPS: Conditioned Responses | *Zack Curry*	
	Comparing	106
	Copying	110
	Competing	113
8	FORWARDING	
	RSVP	120
	Forwarding	123
	Up Ahead	127

Appendix—GUIDES

	A. Community/Small Group Guide	130
	B. Coaching Questions and Guide	133

Resources—LEADER BREAKTHRU

	The Leadership Development Series	139
	Focused Living, APEX, and Resonance	140

before words: *Terry*

There are no times without choices.
    —Henri Nouwen

To be alive is to be vulnerable.
    —Madeleine L'Engle

There is within each of us a holy longing.

Something each of us desires to see and live into. It has been placed there before time began. It will not go away despite all of the ploys of culture to drown it out. It is a desire to be part of something larger—beyond any one person. Merton tells us that it requires heroic humility to discover and move into that life of meaning and purpose.

Surrender and alignment are the doors that open up a life to the sovereign purposes of Christ. What's required is what Church history has referred to as a time of awakening. A time when the heart takes the lead, and life is lived not because it all makes sense, but because of this sovereign design.

There is a good chance you've picked up this book because that same holy discontent has surfaced in your life. Many before you have gone through this same Awakening Transition. Ahead are choices, new ways to view yourself and the Lord, and a vulnerability that births a deeper, more authentic faith. Having had the honor to walk alongside many who have gone before you, my prayer is that these words will used, in part, to help you awaken to the call of God on your life.

Terry Walling
Chico, CA
August 2014

before words: *Kyle*

*Wake up, sleeper, rise from the dead,
and Christ will shine on you.*
—Ephesians 5:14

Several months before I took a leap of faith during my own Awakening Transition, a man I didn't know came up to me at church one Sunday, handed me a 3" x 5" index card with some scribbling on it, and, without saying a word, promptly returned to his seat. The inscription on the card said this:

You have been on an uphill climb...You have been pulling people with you...BUT get ready...You are about to top the hill. When you do... watch out and hang on for the ride of your life!!!

Though I never did get a chance to talk with the man who gave me the card, he couldn't have been more right. The Awakening Transition is a fight, an uphill battle, a gauntlet—and it's even more beautiful, poetic, and awe-inspiring then the sunrise on the cover of this book. Not because everything is roses and lilies on the other side, but because of whom God proves himself to be over and over again: all that is good, all that is faithful, all that is love.

For you who would pick up this book with a burning desire in your heart to live a life that matters, a life in obedient pursuit of God, my prayer and exhortation for you is simple:
Surrender. Believe. Persevere. Fight!

Kyle Walling
Chico, CA
August 2014

before words: *Zack*

Contributing to this project has been a great honor. I have experienced first-hand the benefits of having community—
fathers, mothers, and a coach—walk with me through the journey of leadership, in the midst of transitions, feeling stuck or even unsure of the purpose God has for your life. I still remember sitting down with Terry for the first time, feeling hopeless, confused, and a bit lost. The breakthrough I experienced not only was the beginning of one of the most significant transitions in my life, but it also gave me even more resolve to "give away" and help leaders facing the very things that I was.

Terry is an amazing friend and coach. I am eternally grateful for his investment in me. My prayer is that this journey will leave you with fresh hope, perspective, and clarity to the purposes of God for your life. After all, what God wants to do through your life is much more significant than you may realize, because, in the end, it is about giving it away to the world around you.

Zack Curry
Sacramento, CA
September 2014

introduction

This book is for those who hunger to live a life that counts and make a difference. It is not for the passive or undecided, but for those who are making the choice to step over the line to discover all of what God has designed for them and their lives. It is for those who are awakening to the calling of God on their lives.

Awakening is about God's call on a Christ-follower's life. This experience can be gradual or radical. It can take place through everyday events and extraordinary moments. It occurs to those who trust in Christ whether he or she operates in the Church, the business sector, the neighborhood, or the campus. It is for the one who desires to deepen his or her love and intimacy with Christ, and to intentionally live like Christ. The goal of this book is to provide greater definition to the stirring and awakening occurring in the hearts of those discovering God's voice in new ways, and those seeking to clarify His purposes for their lives.

God shapes our lives over our lifetimes. He does some of His greatest shaping work during times of transition. Awakening is a time of transition, an in-between moment in the journey of a Christ-follower. While most of us want out of these confusing times, God wants in. These are often the Potter's greatest moments—sculpting influence and revealing destiny— the unfolding of a life direction, and God's ongoing shaping work to those who choose to surrender to God's sovereign plans.

In your hands is the product of 20 years of coaching those who are experiencing God's shaping work during this first of three major life transitions: the Awakening Transition. This book also draws upon over 40 years of research related to the personal development of risk-taking, Kingdom leaders and Christ-followers just like yourself. Underneath these coaching insights rests the analysis of over 5,000 biblical, historical, and contemporary leaders, completed by J. Robert Clinton, author of the book, *The Making of a Leader*.

The design of *Awakening* is three-fold:

1. To be used as a self-discovery guide for individuals to better understand the unique place and time in their journey where God clarifies calling and life direction

2. To be a coaching resource used by both coach and coachee to help them walk together through this important time of transition (see Appendix, pp. 133-138).

3. To be a small group discussion resource, guiding the interaction and insights of those who are walking together, seeking how God is at work in each of their lives (see Appendix, pp. 130-132).

Awakening focuses on issues related to personal calling and life direction. The difference between knowing what God wants and breaking through to new behavior is coaching. We highly recommend you process both these concepts and this time in your life with others. You do not get to clarity alone. The "come alongside relationship" is crucial. If you need help finding a personal coach to help you process this time, Leader Breakthru can help you find one right for you. (www.leaderbreakthru.com/coach-me)

Awakening is one of three books that make up the Leadership Development Series from Leader Breakthru. Each of these books aims to serve as a guide in the navigation of the three important times of transition that all Christ-followers face. These three transitions were first introduced in my earlier book, *Stuck! Navigating the Transitions of Life & Leadership*. Each of these three books takes a deeper look at one of the following three transitions: the Awakening Transition, the Deciding Transition, and the Finishing Transition. (www.leaderbreakthru.com/leadership-development-series)

The Awakening Transition often surfaces somewhere in the 20s or 30s of a Christ-follower, though it is not uncommon for those in their 40s to need to visit (or revisit) personal calling in order to gain greater clarity on one's identity and life direction. This transition seeks to build voice recognition and the identification of the Shepherd's shaping work related to a Christ-follower's influence. Two core discovery tools aid one's ability to navigate the Awakening Transition: a personal timeline and a statement of personal calling. The timeline provides lifetime perspective, while the calling statement becomes a compass for the future. Coaching and the context of a Christian community both help to ensure that exciting insights are able to transfer into new, concrete steps forward.

In *Stuck!*, I introduced the Transition Life Cycle to help us understand how transitions work and what can be anticipated as one is processing a transition. The Awakening Transition will follow this same, generic pathway.

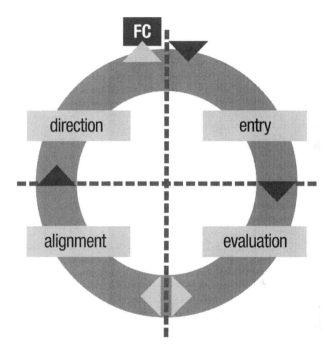

As a Christ-follower moves from entry to new direction, the largest part of the Awakening Transition will be a time of evaluation and alignment. As the transition moves back and forth between these two stages, God does some of His most important work aligning our hearts with His plans.

ON A PERSONAL NOTE

I started out writing this book by creating a fictitious leader facing the Awakening Transition who was a composite of the many of the leaders I've coached through the years. The more I wrote, however, the more I realized that in many ways I was describing the Awakening Transition that my son Kyle has experienced.

At the time of this writing, Kyle serves as a pastor to college and high school students in Chico, CA. Kyle and his wife Megan have a deep-seated commitment to their own formation and the formation of others as they look to share Jesus' way of life in the places they inhabit each day. Their journey has taken them from full-time graphic design, into their current position described later in this book, and beyond. I felt it was important to share parts of their story in the pages ahead not because they always got it right or because everyone who goes through the Awakening Transition moves into vocational ministry, as was the end-result for them. Instead, I did so because the narrative of their transition is just one example of how God awakens us to discover and live out His call on our lives. I am very grateful that Kyle and Megan have allowed me to share some of what he experienced during his Awakening Transition.

Kyle's experiences provide helpful illustrations of what passionate, Christ-followers face through this time of transition. While I've used much of their stories, please know that I have also taken liberty with them in order to teach and illustrate some core leader development concepts. At times, some of our conversations have been generalized and adjusted to better fit with the more generic understanding of the Awakening Transition. Also note that Kyle's journal entries found throughout the book serve as his reflective commentary as one walking through this transition.

Zack Curry is a friend and leader who I have also helped through the Awakening Transition. His insights come from processing his transition, as well as from years of ministry experience. At the time of this writing, Zack serves with Jesus Culture, a ministry in Sacramento, CA, that provides oversight of a new church full of young leaders, all passionate for Christ and seeking to better clarify their own personal callings.

As you read this book, it is my prayer that these stories and insights will stir something up inside you, throwing you deeper into abandonment for Christ and increasing your passion to live out His call on your life. It is my prayer that you will experience new clarity and a fresh new work of God's revealing Spirit in your life. Knowledge and insights alone about this time of transition will not be enough. I pray that you allow God to take you from where you are to a new place in your passion for Him. I desire that He kindle (or re-kindle) a deeper awareness of His sovereign designs for your life, along with the courage necessary to trust Him for more.

God's calling on your life is there, though often buried under the trappings of culture, the expectations of others, and even under some of your own ambitions. It is my hope that this book helps you discover the calling that has been written into your heart by the Triune God before time began (Ephesians 2:10).

Terry Walling

COMMON QUESTIONS SURROUNDING THE AWAKENING TRANSITION:

- What do I really want out of life?
- Which way do I go?
- Which option is best for me?
- What is my calling?
- What is the purpose of my life? Of life in general?
- Do I have to decide it all right now?
- What is my vision for the future?
- What is truly important to me?
- Why is the way ahead not more clear?
- How do I choose?
- What is God saying to me?
- How do I know that what I chose is right?
- What does God really want from me?
- How do I know God will be there to provide for me?
- What if I fail?
- Why can't I catch a break?
- Why does it take so long for God to reveal His plans?
- When will someone give me a shot?
- What if I get what I want? Will I be happy?

THOUGHTS RELATED TO THE AWAKENING TRANSITION:

We were meant to live for so much more
Have we lost ourselves?
Somewhere we live inside
Somewhere we live inside
We were meant to live for so much more
Have we lost ourselves?
Somewhere we live inside
Somewhere we live inside

—Switchfoot, "Meant to Live"

introduction

We have been set up for a crisis in identity. We come into the world longing to be known and with a deep-seated fear that we aren't what we should be...Most of us are living out a script that someone else has written for us.

—Brent Curtis and John Eldredge, *The Sacred Romance*

Accepting identity with Jesus has a reverse side. It also means rejecting identity gained by the approval of the crowd.

—James Houston, *The Transforming Power of Prayer*

Two basic emotions go with awakening: it is both a comfort and a threat. It is comfort because there is a sense of awakening to deeper realities of who we are and who God is. But at the same time there is threat: in that awakening, we recognize that we are not who we ought to be and that God is something far more than we thought.

—M. Robert Mulholland, *Invitation to a Journey*

1

invitation

*Left to ourselves, we can never handle our own uniqueness.
We have to give the burden of being me to God's care and nurture.*

—JAMES HOUSTON, *THE TRANSFORMING POWER OF PRAYER*

*We push ourselves to wield influence or make a mark. Often we
call that "vocation" but Jesus calls it "temptation." He has no patience with the one who insists he jump from the temple to show his
power or turn stones into bread to prove his ministry credentials.
He has heard God speak of his belovedness as God's Son. That
forms the basis of what he does and knows himself called to do.*

—HENRI NOUWEN, *TURN MY MOURNING INTO DANCING*

*We must attune ourselves to unexpected movements of grace,
which do not fit our own preconceived ideas of the spiritual life at
all. And which in no way flatter our own ambitious aspirations.*

—THOMAS MERTON, *SPIRITUAL DIRECTION AND MEDITATION*

As Jesus walked beside the Sea of Galilee, he saw Simon and his brother Andrew casting a net into the lake, for they were fishermen. "Come, follow me," Jesus said, "and I will send you out to fish for people." At once they left their nets and followed him. When he had gone a little farther, he saw James son of Zebedee and his brother John in a boat, preparing their nets. Without delay he called them, and they left their father Zebedee in the boat with the hired men and followed him (Mark 1:16-20).

A NARRATIVE

"We need you!"

"We want you to be part of our team!"

"We would like to offer you a job."

Finally! The breakthrough. These words are golden for anyone hungering to get out of the mundane, for anyone waiting to finally get a chance to move into something more significant. It's like the clouds are opening up and you can feel the warmth of the sun for the first time. For a young leader I had been coaching, the offer of a hoped-for place to belong was just that. And the offer came more than just in time.

His final years of college felt irrelevant—just passing the time, waiting on a degree he doubted that he really needed. He often wondered how his schoolwork related to what he knew he really wanted to do with his life. To receive an offer to join a company that valued him and knew what he could offer—not to mention in a field in which he had skills—all felt too good to be true. He knew it didn't always happen like this, so it felt like something deeper was going on. He had been praying for God to lead his way forward.

Patience had never been this individual's strong suit; it's just not how he was made. Life had been lived in "hurry up" mode and it always seemed important for him to live one step ahead. So, coming to terms with waiting, and then not knowing what he was really supposed to do with his life, had not been easy. In truth, he knew very little about where he was ultimately heading; he just knew he was tired of waiting and that there had to be something more on the horizon. His instincts were telling him that he was facing an important moment, but not the final answer. He was looking for some kind of sign that God was working and leading. He had surrendered his life to Christ. But what did God really want him to do?

The new job seemed like that sign. It meant a geographical move. The scenery would change from the familiar to a world of new and different. That felt exciting and good. Out there might be some of his answers—his answers for where his life was headed. But he needed another set of eyes to look it all over. Again, it was as if it was all too good to be true. Had God really moved in and opened the way forward? Was Christ at work in all of this? Was He confirming his call to the marketplace, to use his skills in graphic design in the corporate world?

As one who has the privilege of coaching people like Kyle, I enjoyed sitting back and celebrating this new opportunity. Some of those I coach face important times of decision—crossroads moments in one's life where that person is being challenged to walk down previously unknown paths. Almost all of those I walk alongside want to gain greater "voice recognition" of Christ. They are seeking to clarify issues of direction and life purpose. The more that answers don't come, the more their frustration builds, and the more they turn to people like me. They are passionate to sense God's direction for their lives, but are often confused by the delays and the waiting. When answers finally do come, they are often relieved and excited, but can find themselves wondering if this is God really leading—or if this will lead to what they really want.

The offer had come just in time. (And, by the way, the offer rarely comes early.) As we looked back over his life, it seemed as if the Lord always took Kyle right down to the last minute. Just when something needed to happen, or when it looked like nothing would ever happen, something did: a person comes along, a new option surfaces, a clear path opens up, a new opportunity presents itself, etc.

Kyle hungered for a clear sense of direction not only concerning a job, but also in terms of what God had in mind for his future. He had prayed, yet for many months answers seemed to be slow in coming. Like most, he struggled with all the waiting. But one good thing about Kyle was that he was determined to not make a move forward without knowing his next steps were in line with God's desires, at least as best as he could determine.

As we sat together at a local coffee shop, I read through the proposal. Jobs like the one being offered were hard to land right out of college. In this offer, though, it all seemed to have come together. The warm sun breaking through the hazy clouds overhead was almost a sign that the breakthrough he needed had come. Though Kyle was ready to start tomorrow, jump ship, skip all the graduation stuff, and get on with this next step, he also wanted to be sure.

"So, what do you think?" he asked. "Does it all look okay?"

"I think it all looks pretty great!" I replied.

"It's a incredible way to start out," he said. "A job like this right out of the chute is amazing!"

"It all looks really good to me, bud, especially in light of how God has been at work in your journey!"

I went on to explain: "It feels to me like you are being invited into a great job, but also something more than just a job. Yeah, the job is what a lot of people would kill for, but I sense that the Lord is honoring your earlier decisions to chase the passion of your heart, not just land a job. The guys running this company are Christians. They have a passion for seeing their skills and abilities be used for the Kingdom. And they know that what God wants for you is important to you. I'm pretty excited!"

"I think you're right," said Kyle. "I feel like this is the beginning of something. I'm not quite sure where all of this is heading, but it feels like God is opening this door, wanting me to trust Him and follow where He may want to take my life."

I sat back and watched as Kyle processed the moment, realizing that something more was at play. We both knew that this moment was the beginning of other important moments ahead: God was taking the lead and Kyle knew the job was a front for more that was yet to unfold.

Kyle took the job.

He soon discovered that this moment launched him into a time of transition—a time of awakening. The job was God's invitation to something more. It was the beginning of the journey to unfold God's unique call on his life. The choice of the job would become the way the Lord would take him down a different path. He would later be surprised at the outcome. But first steps begin somewhere. Christ had begun to speak deep into Kyle's heart, "Come follow me," and the door had opened. Kyle was being called to a new place. His life—like each of our lives—is profoundly shaped by moments just like these. It is just how

God does things. Life decisions often are about more than just jobs, or decisions about college, or the choice of a spouse. We are meant to live for so much more and God uses people, events, and circumstances to shape our lives. More on that later.

SOME THOUGHTS

Many of us have heard stories like Kyle's. Some of us have even lived a similar narrative. Most of us have read the account of when the early disciples became disciples. All us have been through moments of waiting, wanting life direction to clarify, and struggling with answers that have not yet come. Whether around the table at your local coffee shop or on the distant shores of the Sea of Galilee, awakening occurs as Jesus moves into our lives and asks for control. The time of first awakening is always about issues of control, trust, and risk. Can God be trusted, and will we risk that uncertainty and follow?

I continue to be stunned by how quickly these early disciples responded to Christ's invitation. Are you? The abandonment of all they knew, their willingness to follow the One they had barely met, and all that they did not know in route to finding the life they knew not of, until they found it. It's big.

I marvel similarly at all the moments I have had the privilege of witnessing when Christ-followers make choices to respond to God's voice and align their lives to what Christ wants. I have the incredible honor of listening to their hearts come alive as they awaken to God's sovereign, shaping work. Moments like these are defining moments. Life changes. Moving from living according to what others expect for our lives, and what culture has shaped it to be, to what God has designed before time began.

Make no mistake: the moments of awakening and calling can be both exciting and threatening. These are the moments in which all of life changes. Jesus' invitation is not to join a religion. His call is not to imitate what others have done, and he wants nothing to do with turning us into church attenders alone. God seeks to awaken each of our hearts to an important discovery: that each of our lives has an eternal destiny and purpose far beyond the navigating of life's key decisions.

Jesus could have focused his calling on those known to be religious and devoted. His call could have gone out to the studied ones, the masters of the law, the zealots, the ceremonially committed. But his invitation was extended to a different tribe: the hungry and the honest, those who know they were in need of a leader, the sick, the hurting, the emotionally scarred, those needing a physician. And Jesus continues to call people just like those who first responded. People like you and I, who work in the marketplace, live in neighborhoods, walk on campus, live in the trenches, and whose pedigree is a different kind of life. We are the overlooked and unnoticed. Jesus bypassed the obvious in order to call those he wanted (Mark 3:13). He goes after the authentic, those who dare to be themselves before him. He craves people who are the non-pretenders. He went after those who would have the courage to break free and follow.

For most, Christ's call to "Follow me" rings with familiarity, but it's essential to remember that Jesus "called" the disciples to simply follow life as he prescribed. To be more than just those who attend religious gathering. He summons us to community and an experience of a life that would imitate his life—a life of intimacy and dependence on the will of the Father. This life is countercultural to what all of us who follow had known and lived. Jesus framed this life when he called his first disciples: "Jesus went up on a mountainside and called to him those he wanted, and they came to him. He appointed twelve that they might be with him and that he might send them out to preach and to have authority to drive out demons" (Mark 3:13-15).

The life for Christ must first be experienced with Christ. Awakening is first and foremost a call to experience Christ and a life of intimacy with him before it is a call to do work for him. It is a call "to" someone, before it is a call to "do" something. Whether clothed in Kyle's stepping into the right job or the disciples stepping away from their familiar, right from the start, Jesus signaled that the source of our lives would be our journey into him. The awakening and the call are not about ambition; they're about alignment and relationship.

Christ's calling is not the build of lasting institutions, the penning of a theological treatise, or the need to re-brand the religion of the day. Jesus came to model a life of intimacy with the Father, and life that was possible, lived out each day between the Father, Son, and Spirit. We too can enter that kind of intimacy and relationship. Matthew 3:17 states, "This is my beloved son in whom I am well pleased." Our calling is an awakening to that same unconditional love that stands on a seashore, or whispers behind a potential new job: *Let me love you in a way you've never known, and with a power that will change you and the world in which you live.*

We know the response of the fishermen was immediate:

"At once they left."

They left all they knew about "life" in search of life. Immediate detachment. Separation from all that was known up and accepted up to that point. Walking away from all that their culture had programmed them to be and to do. At once, they left all their security, even leaving family and friends standing in the boat, and followed. And along the way, this same response of surrender and alignment would be called for again. It was Simon Peter who answered Jesus question of whether they too would desert him, "'Lord, to whom shall we go? You have the words of eternal life'" (John 6:68).

Why do men and women today respond to this call from Christ in a similar way? It is because Christ-followers begin to discover that their hearts have become sovereignly sensitized, designed to respond the moment they brush up against their sense of destiny. Calling is not something you invent; it is something you discover. It surfaces each time we hear the whispers of the Triune God and catch a glimpse of the plans etched long ago. Calling propels a life forward. It is a hunger to know who we are and what God has for us to do. Calling is about intimacy, and the good deeds that God authored before time began (Psalm 139: 13-16; Ephesians 2:8-10). The Life-Giver awakens hearts and lives to experience true life, and all that it means.

You and I were never meant to live for a job, a title, or the things we can possess or accomplish. You and I were meant to live for so much more: to know Christ in all His fullness and out of that union to participate in displaying life as He designed it.

Are you ready?

Christ could be extending this very same invitation to you today.

It is a call on your life much bigger than your current plans, or what you can possibly dream.

It's an awakening to something more.

You were meant to live for so much more.

At end of the next chapter, we'll pause for some reflection on all of this.

UNTANGLING

The focus of the Awakening Transition is that of direction, identity, and personal calling. To understand the idea of calling, it must first be untangled. Compare the following statements with your current understanding of calling. Is this how you see calling?

- Calling is sourced in an individual's passion for greater relationship and intimacy with Christ.
- Calling is dynamic and shaped over time. It unfolds over a lifetime as one seeks to live in relationship with Christ—and love Him to the end.
- Our "first order" call to is to be before it is a call to do.
- Calling is much more than vocation, with each of us called into a life of ministry.
- Calling applies to all Christ-followers.
- The Lord sculpts calling, as opposed to us seeking to respond to what God has done for us, and the ambition that it can subtly produce.
- God sculpts callings as he allows the people, events, and circumstances to reveal our place and role in His Kingdom.
- Calling is discovered, not invented. It is birthed with others, in the context of community and ministry, and is the product of obedience.
- Calling serves as a compass, setting the true north of a life and day-to-day direction.

How'd you do? Is this what you know calling to be? Take a few moments and go back and review the statements above.

In his book *The Call*, Os Guinness documents an historical view of calling—a view in line with that of this book. It was the puritans belief and understanding that calling extends to all Christians—not just to a separate clergy. For them, calling is endowed to each believer at the point of conversion. Every follower of Jesus is "called" into ministry and over his or her lifetime is entrusted with a personal call to ministry and to live for Christ, regardless of training, gifting, or position.

The Puritans subscribed to the notion that each life had, and was to be lived, with a sense of sovereign call and purpose. Guinness summarizes:

> Our primary calling as followers of Christ is by him, to him and for him. First and foremost we are called to Someone (God), not to something (such as motherhood, politics, or teaching) or to somewhere (such as the inner city or Outer Mongolia) (p. 31).
>
> Our secondary calling, considering who God is as sovereign, is that everyone, everywhere, and everything should think, speak, live and act entirely for him (p. 31).

Calling is a God-birthed and God-inspired mandate on a life, seared deep into the longings of a heart before time began, shaped into existence by God Himself, and intended for expression to a world separated from God. It is a description of a Christ-follower's unique life purpose. Clarity on one's calling becomes like a compass that guides and directs future decision-making. Calling defines "true north" and sets a life on a path to be lived out.

In the Awakening Transition, God begins the process of stirring the soul to give clarity on one's call. Passions are ignited, deep desires are made known and a course begins to emerge, often revealing a different life trajectory. New passion and devotion comes not out of obligation or duty now, but out of wanting to live a life that counts. Living true to this new passion also begins to build greater self-awareness and clarity in one's identity. No longer known by our families of birth, our status in society, our job we hold, or the accumulation of wealth, we are known by Who we know: we are now sons and daughters of the King named Jesus, and we serve His kingdom, not our own. The Church groans and limps along today because we have locked up the concept of calling into a corner called vocational ministry and, thus, bound the hands of a struggling Church that is far greater than she has ever exhibited.

In the Awakening Transition, the follower learns that Christ's voice can and must be recognized, sometimes even above those who claim to represent Him. His voice is not in the wind, earthquake, or fire, but in the still small voice (1 Kings 19:11-12).

One final comment about the time of awakening and personal calling. In the Awakening Transition, it is not uncommon to hear expressions of both excitement and passion joined together with doubts and feelings of personal inadequacy. This wide range of emotions can confuse those who want to follow Christ into a new place, making them feel that they are not qualified, that their pasts disqualify them, and that their abilities are lacking. These responses are not any different from those we see in Scripture. The prophet Isaiah's voiced these same personal disqualifications: "I am a man of unclean [unworthy] lips" (Isaiah 6:5). Jeremiah also doubted his worthiness, crying out that he was too young and not qualified for such a call (Jeremiah 1:6-9). And Paul called Timothy to not despise his young age (1 Timothy 4:12). It should come as no surprise, then, that those whose hearts are awakened to Christ's call are prime targets for the Enemy to sow doubts and intimidation.

Calling provides direction. It is the summation for a Christ-follower of where God is leading his or her life and how God has shaped his or her life and ministry. It is a compass that helps steer future decision-making in the days ahead. We will discuss the concept of calling later in the book.

THINKING IT OVER
You | One-to-One | Coaching | Group

Below is a guide to help you better process what you've just read. It can be used as you review the ideas personally, as a one-to-one discussion tool, as a small group interaction guide, or as a resource for a coaching conversation between you and a personal development coach.

If you are using *Awakening* with a small group, the following provides reflection questions for your first group conversation.

Reflect on the following quote:

Left to ourselves, we can never handle our own uniqueness. We have to give the burden of "being me" to God's care and nurture.

—James Houston, *The Transforming Power of Prayer*

Reflect on the following biblical text:

Psalm 62

Reflect on the following questions:

- Review the questions on page 14. Which of these come closest to some of the questions you're currently asking?
- How is the biblical narrative similar to and/or different from how God calls people today?
- How might have those early disciples felt? How do you feel as you consider that God may be laying claim to your life?
- What's similar and what's different in terms of your thinking as you read the summary statements regarding calling?
- What do you hear related to your own calling? What might God be doing in your life?

WANT MORE?

Here is a link to Leader Breakthru's Website that will take you further on topics covered in this chapter:

www.leaderbreakthru.com/stuck-the-book

2
entry

I don't ask you to bless what I have decided to do, but give me the grace to discover and live out what you have dreamed for me.

—MACRINA WIEDERKEHR, *SEASONS OF YOUR HEART*

Yes, there is that voice, the voice that speaks from above and from within that whispers softly or declares loudly, "You are my Beloved, on you my favor rests." It is certainly is not easy to hear that voice in a world filled with voices that shout: You are no good, you are worthless; you are despicable, you are nobody— unless you can demonstrate the opposite. These negative voices are so loud and persistent that it's easy to believe them. That's the great trap. It is the trap of self-rejection.

—HENRI NOUWEN, *LIFE OF THE BELOVED*

SOMETHING MORE

Those early days of Kyle's new job were good days.

Lots of different!

Kyle found himself working with talented people, and it was just plain fun for him to finally break into a world and make a contribution with his skills and abilities in a way that he had really wanted to for some time.

He had gotten married and then moved to Texas, where he was being groomed by a gifted graphic designer, learning a lot, and working for a company and team that shared similar visions, passions, and interests. Everything in his world felt good and right once more.

As the first few days turned into the first few years, things began to settle into a good rhythm. His first year of apprenticeship had concluded and new graphic design responsibilities and duties were now his responsibility. Daily tasks and projects kept him busy. The work and the initial deadlines were all pretty much as he expected. The job had its demands, but they were wanted. He wanted to carve out a place for himself. And he did.

While it was good to see that Kyle was in his "field" and was working with good people, he was experiencing the demands of a growing company. Soon, he was getting pigeonholed into doing what he could do, but not what he was passionate about doing. He knew he was the new kid on the block—the low one on the totem pole. He got that! He also knew that every job had its less-than-fun side. But the further he went, the further he found himself from his passion to create and was instead being relegated to the monotony of production work. No matter what he voiced, he was confronted with the reality of work! Some around him could see what was happening, but nothing really changed. He was feeling more and more trapped.

Kyle and Megan began attending a church that had an active ministry in the area of small groups, a heart for missions, and a passion to mentor leaders. Before they knew it, Kyle and Megan were launching a small group of their own, and Kyle himself was receiving some incredible mentoring from the small groups pastor. Kyle and Megan loved their group. They loved the chance to share in life and ministry with others. And they loved that they were able to find a church that felt more like them and their passions. It only lasted for the short duration of Kyle's apprenticeship with the company, since it ended as they headed off to Arizona for a graduate program for Megan, but they knew that this would prove to be a significant experience for the rest of their lives.

Kyle was incredibly grateful for the start in the workplace in his passion area of graphic design, but the dream of the first year was now fading, diminishing under the tyranny of the urgent. His clients wanted him to simply "make things look nice" as opposed to do real creative work. He was watching himself become resigned to just doing the work and then looking forward to weekends and extended time off. That wasn't why he had signed up for all of this. All of what he had dreamed about was becoming a distant memory to him and for him.

He was left wondering if this is how life really is, at least when it came to "making a living": that there is no perfect job. Should he just buck up and realize this was how it was going to be? Are these the "dues" he must pay to provide for his wife and new family? He had heard a recruiter say once that three out of four people don't really love—or even like—what they do professionally.

Maybe this is just how it is—how the "real world" works! Welcome to adulthood, Kyle thought.

Yet, the more he tried to work himself free, just to be able to go on, the more a cloud of confusion settled in. And then, out of nowhere, a realization: *Maybe this was not about my job or my career after all! Maybe something else is going on, and God is trying to get my attention. Maybe all of this is about something more.*

Kyle has great relational skills, but by nature he is an introvert and needs to first process the things within him—and even seek others' thoughts—before he is ready to conclude and share his thinking out loud and try to put all the pieces together. Once he has a chance to hear himself think something through and receive the information he needs, sitting down and working out what God wants is easier. One of the lessons of coaching is to coach the person and how they process information.

SOMETHING ELSE

Kyle knew that I coach a lot of people through transitions. He was beginning to realize that what he was experiencing was something more than just issues related to his job. Kyle needed me to put on the hat of a coach and try to help him sort through what was going on.

Kyle designed the cover of my first book, *Stuck!* We had searched for a graphic representation of what transitions felt like. A fish swimming round and round, trapped in a fishbowl seemed to work. But what we once joked about now felt very different as Kyle found himself the potential subject of his own cover art.

Our first coaching session was about listening as Kyle got all the pieces out on the table and heard himself give voice to all of what he was feeling. Over coffee, I listened and he talked.

"Just talk it through Kyle," I said. "I'm happy to just listen as you process where you're at. And, you may or may not be in a transition. We can discover that together."

"I feel like I keep going round and round on all of this!" he responded. "The more and more I think this through, the more I feel like God may be doing something related to me that I hadn't seen earlier."

I began listening for—and hearing—some of the characteristics and themes that typically emerge when someone is in a transition. But what I think is not nearly as important as what God might be saying to the person sitting across from me.

"Okay!" I intervened. "Tell me what you're beginning to see—and what you think might be going on!"

For the next few minutes, Kyle began to unpack his summation of what he thought God might be doing. "I loved the job, the people, the chance to do what I dreamed of, and the chance to make a contribution with a group of people I respected," he started. "I thought landing the job was my answer. And in some ways it was."

He went on.

"I also know that I needed to be patient and allow myself to learn and grow into this new position. I was the new kid on the block and, in some sense, needed to pay my dues."

I watched and listened as Kyle began to take things deeper.

"I know that patience has never been a strength of mine, but for awhile I was okay and really content to just allow things to unfold. It was all going well, but I could sense that underneath, God was working with me in the area of trust. It was as if He was testing me to see if I would really trust Him, not just with my future, but with the future of my family. And would I trust him when I can't see where he is leading? Even though I had landed a good job, was this really what I was meant to do?"

I decided it was important to synthesize where we were. "So, even though things were good—even from the beginning—there are still some questions?" I asked.

"Yeah, I think so!" said Kyle.

He continued, "They weren't questions about whether I did the right thing related to accepting the job or the company I joined. The questions were ones within me! They had to do with where all of this was leading."

I could tell that Kyle had touched on something important. Sometimes, good things—even right things—can still mean there are questions related to best things or a greater thing that God may be at work doing. God shapes each of our lives over a lifetime. Each step builds on the last. You can feel right about something, but also know there's more. We Christ-followers want certainty from our God, but He continually offers us new insights and clarity. Again, more about all of this later.

The farther Kyle went down the road of unpacking his thinking, the more a pattern began to emerge. What once appeared to be the answer to frustrations—and eventually the beginning of something new—now had become a signal of something more. Landing the job had actually served to launch a transition, the Awakening Transition. In reality, the landing of the job was actually the beginning of the "in between."

"So what do you hear yourself saying, Kyle, as you unpack all of this? What do you think all of this might mean?" I asked.

"That's why came to you!" he responded. "What are you hearing?"

Discovery is the key to ownership. What individuals discover, they own. What we own, we have a greater potential to take responsibility for to solve. My role as his coach was to first ask Kyle to draw his own conclusions before I gave him my feedback.

"I've got some thoughts," I said, "but first I want to hear what you think."

After a few minutes of silence, Kyle responded. "From everything I can see, it feels like I'm in a transition. And though this job has gone relatively well, it feels like God is not done speaking to me about what He wants or where He could be leading me."

"I agree," I said. "But it's important for you to first hear yourself say it."

"What I think is one thing—and I know you respect my opinion," I went on, "but what you think at this point is really the most important thing. If you can resolve inside of you that God is still at work here—even though we thought we had our answer with the job—then you will be more open to go with Him as He seeks to lead you to the answer." I could tell that as hard it was to come to that realization, it was really as true assessment of what God was doing.

Transitions can often last between three months and three years, so I went on to talk about how transitions take time and are much more than momentary blips in God's shaping work. Transitions aren't always easy, but when Christ-followers look back, they realize what has been happening. His is the job to lead. Ours is to follow.

 THE BACK STORY: DIRECTION

Kyle's transition began long before he knew it. Its beginnings were back even in his later college years and his growing frustrations. Though he thought he was heading out on a new adventure in the area of his career, God was actually using the job to begin Kyle's awakening to His desires for his life.

God uses people, events, and circumstances to shape our lives. He uses transitions to reveal issues of life purpose and direction. Kyle thought he had that purpose and direction, but he was really just beginning to set his compass to true north! God was awakening him to the calling He had planted deep within his heart.

Entry into the Awakening Transition—as with any transition—is very much like what you just read. Uncertainty often hits, bringing with it a sense of restlessness and confusion. Answers are few, questions abound, and we are often well into a time of transition before we realize it. Transitions are more than just a time of confusion. Something very different is occurring. We are often faced with the reality that God is orchestrating something else, but in the beginning, there is little clue as to what the future might hold. God is often arranging and re-arranging our plans to better conform them to His own.

DIRECTION

Our culture has taught us to link influence with position. We've been told that the careers we pursue and/or the jobs we hold are the keys to the difference we can make. One of the key voices we listen to in our culture is the voice of occupation.

Though we've seen examples to the contrary (e.g., Mother Teresa, Brother Lawrence, etc.), we are so steeped in this cultural lie that we in the West still chase the myth. It helps us feel "normal" to adopt this belief, so it is pursued day-in and day-out with little question. We who love Christ are not exempt. We will move in step with this belief unless confronted by a sovereign interruption called a "transition." We also elevate some occupations more than others, giving those who hold these positions greater influence over our lives.

Here are some familiar examples:

- "The president seems to think we should…"
- "The speaker at a recent conference said…"
- "N.T. Wright says…"
- "My professor from college says…"
- "Scientists tell us…"
- "The CEO of a Fortune 500 company said…"

We listen. We value. We esteem positional voices as more important than other voices, serving to only reinforce the role of position in our lives. In fact, this pathology has led me to want to listen to—and gain the approval of—the voices of people in these positions even more than God's. What you think of me and what those in authority have thought of me has often become more important than what God has clearly declared about me.

Okay—but what's the point here? Doesn't everybody need a job? The Awakening Transition is about more than a job. It's a time of awakening to the call that God places on every Christ-follower's life. It is the first act of a narrative that from this point forward unfolds into a unique, Kingdom contribution. Calling is more about our influence and our identity than our vocation. Culture has tuned us to seek a job. God has shaped our lives for a purpose and a sense of destiny. In this sense, it's countercultural. In Christ's economy, we are called to a place of influence, as opposed to title or position.

Ours is the call to follow Christ. Christ lived the life of greatest influence, yet he held no position. The Awakening Transition has to do with the call of God for each of us to move beyond the shallow pursuit of position in order to adopt the idea of Kingdom influence. Right off the bat, calling means the choice of a different path: the choice to discover how we are meant to live for so much more.

Jesus Christ modeled this life every day he walked this earth. Philippians 2 talks about his conscious laying laid down of his rights to position, power, acclaim, and title. The power that drove his life was, instead, the revelation he received daily from the Father, a result of his ongoing, daily surrender. Scripture is clear that Jesus' influence was a result of his intimacy with the Father. In his humanity, we learn that the prize of surrender is revelation. We learn in John 5:19, "the Son can do nothing by himself; he can do only what he sees his Father doing, because whatever the Father does the Son also does." Influence is not a result of position, but submission to and alignment with God's purposes.

The Awakening Transition readies a Christ-follower for the process of discovery. Calling is about life direction and the setting of a divine compass situated deeper within the heart of a believer, providing an internal GPS that starts to inform future decision-making.

Calling is also a summation statement, providing a Christ-follower with his or her best-understanding-to-date of his or her God-authored influence—the good deeds placed within our narratives before time began (Ephesians 2:10). God has always been at work shaping this influence into our lives. The real question is whether each of us makes the choice to align with His work and purposes. In the Awakening Transition, God strikes at the heart of the first major issue and obstacle a Christ-follower must face: Does our value come from the position we hold, the titles we gain, and the careers we choose, or does it come from the identity placed deep within the fabric of our lives when we each were "fearfully and wonderfully made" (Psalm 139:14)?

For an example of this, let's turn to Brother Lawrence, a Carmelite monk who lived in France in the 17th century. His approach to life was recounted in his short book, *The Practice of the Presence of God*. The witness of his life has radically impacted the thinking of many throughout Church history, especially on this issue of position, since he daily practiced his allegiance to Christ by washing pots and pans in the monastery kitchen. By loving Christ daily and by aligning his life with Christ's view of him, he served so many as he ministered from his kitchen cathedral.

Here are a few of his thoughts:

- "We ought not to be weary of doing little things for the love of God, who regards not the greatness of the work, but the love with which it is performed."

- "Let us think often that our only business in this life is to please God. Perhaps all besides is but folly and vanity."

- "That there needed neither art nor science for going to God, but only a heart resolutely determined to apply itself to nothing but Him, or for His sake, and to love Him only."

The Awakening Transition is an invitation to a journey and discovery that often gets entangled in voices other than Christ's. This transition and its questions of life purpose and direction are often usurped by the noise of our culture's cry for increased attention and obedience. But even churches at times can muffle what God intends for each and every one who aligns with Christ. The clergy-lay separation has served to create an artificial divide, turning few into performers and the majority into spectators. The confusing, loud noise of entertainment and entitlement has often caused "being in the ministry" to exclusively mean being on the staff of a local church.

Those of you who serve in the marketplace, in the private sector, at home, and in factories that make those things we need each day: you are ones whom God calls into ministry. You look and act just like those Jesus turned to and entrusted his entire movement. If you reach out to your employees and your city with your business, if you're passionate to see the Kingdom come to your neighborhood, if you're active in your children's school, if your heart yearns to bring people together, to live in community, to work, live, play, and pray with others whose call is to live and model a different life that displays the authentic life in Christ, then you are called to minister and live for Christ.

They were two simple words: "Follow me."

What Jesus seems to be saying here is this: *Don't follow what is often modeled and what others may be saying to you. Watch me. Live for me. Live like me. Set a different course. Set your compass to true north.*

Like the words given to a young leader passionate to follow Christ, "For this reason I remind you to fan into flame the gift of God, which is in you" (2 Timothy 1:6).

Live your life aligned more with the creator God than enticing culture.

Live for something more.

Live beyond.

Live for a higher calling.

KYLE'S JOURNAL ENTRY

Looking back, my transition began and was catalyzed by the frustrations and discontentment I felt during my college years. At the time, I was easily frustrated by the fact that I knew God was stirring in my heart a desire for more than the status quo, but I was unable to see where He was taking me—or even what the next step was.

With school, it felt as if there was someone, somewhere, at sometime that had determined "hoops" that everyone had to jump through. And, I like others, I went, kicking and screaming through each one, gaining permission to take one step closer to the "American Dream"—a dream that I was realizing I wanted little to do with.

Writing today with the advantage of several years of perspective, I'm painfully aware of how much I fought and resisted all that God was trying to teach me and how he was trying to form me during that season. Constantly fixated on what was beyond the horizon, I was becoming paralyzed by the mounting frustrations of not being where I wanted to be in life. In all likelihood, "camping" out on this frustration slowed my transition, as God mercifully presented me with opportunity after opportunity—until I finally got it!—and choose to join in on to what He was at work doing.

What I see now is that even in the midst of my own plodding, God was faithful to answer and provide the way forward! The opportunity set before me help break the rigidity of school and take on a job with the ad agency. It all fell right into my lap—almost with no effort on my part. What I had been waiting for was actually unfolding right in front of me! Not only that, but it seemed to come together better than I could have ever planned myself. It felt like someone pressed the fast-forward button and I finally got to where I wanted to be. Realizing that there was a next step brought a deep sense of both relief and excitement within me. It felt like a long time coming, but I was finally was able to move on to a place that I had been ready and waiting for my entire life.

During the year leading up to the job offer, I sensed that God was stretching me in the area of trust. I saw how He invited me to trust Him in new ways, and with more, as He continued to remind me of His faithfulness. As I look at my story, increasing trust seemed to be an important theme for me—a theme that was revisited when all of the excitement for this new opportunity morphed into a time of questioning and a creeping discontentment in my heart.

I sensed that I was still not there—wherever "there" was. That realization came as an unwelcome shock to my system and even brought on a sense of despair and depression. Just about the time I thought I had finally broken through, it seemed like I was back to Square One. So, I set out again, searching for more.

Wrestling resumed in my heart. Will this really all work out? Will I be able to endure more waiting? Maybe I'm supposed to just be satisfied (and grateful) with what I have? How do I really know what God is doing? Wanting? Saying? How is all of this going to work out practically, especially now that I'm married? Now that I have kids? I can't just think about myself now. I have my family to care for.

YOUR JOURNAL ENTRY

Take a moment to write down your thoughts or reactions to this chapter.

THINKING IT OVER

You | One-to-One | Coaching | Group

Below is a guide to help you better process what you've just read. It can be used as you review the ideas personally, as a one-to-one discussion tool, as a small group interaction guide, or as a resource for a coaching conversation between you and a personal development coach.

If you are using *Awakening* with a small group, the following provides reflection questions for your second group conversation.

Reflect on the following quote:

> *Let us think often that our only business in this life is to please God. Perhaps all besides is but folly and vanity.*
>
> —Saint Augustine

Reflect on the following biblical text:

Psalm 86

Reflect on the following questions:

- What sounds familiar to you as you read the first two segments of Kyle's narrative?
- What do you relate to? What is different from your own experience?
- What do you believe Kyle is working through?
- What stands out to you so far about the Awakening Transition?

WANT MORE?

Here is a link to Leader Breakthru's Website that will take you further on topics covered in this chapter:

www.leaderbreakthru.com/awakening/calling

3
evaluation and alignment

Identity does not depend on the role we play or the power it gives us over others. It depends only on the simple fact that we are children of God, valued in and for ourselves.

—PARKER PALMER, *LET YOUR LIFE SPEAK*

The whole of the Christian life is a holy longing. What you desire ardently, as yet you do not see. By withholding of the vision, God extends longing; through longing he extends the soul, by extending he makes room in it. Let us long because we are to be filled...that is our life, to be exercised by longing.

—SAINT AUGUSTINE

NARRATIVE: THE CALL TO SEE

Kyle asked me if we could get some more time together. He felt like he needed some extended time to really lay things out. He wanted me to lead him through a two-day process that I often use with Christ-followers and leaders facing transition moments and needing clarity.

The process I use consists of hearing a leader's life story, identifying key turning points, and then working with them on clarifying two things: first, what God has entrusted to him or her through the various experiences of his or her life and, second, what the past can provide by way of indication as to the direction and future decision-making that he or she will soon face.

"Sure," I said. "How about we book a block of time to walk through the process? We're going to need a few hours!"

Soon, Kyle, Megan, and I met up and began the process of listening to Kyle as he shared his journey so far. Rarely do we stop to articulate our whole life story in one sitting. I could tell that in Kyle there was both hopeful anticipation and nervous uncertainty. He remained hopeful, yet he struggled to see how what was on his heart could actually begin to take shape in his life. Often, emerging leaders become discouraged when there appears to be little or no path to achieving their dreams—and obstacles are many.

Kyle began talking, and I once again did my best to listen intently.

Sharing his entire story in one sitting proved to be a powerful time for Kyle, as it has for many others. It's stunning to listen to how God has been at work, forming and shaping the values of a life and heart. Kyle spent several hours examining his timeline and talking through what he considered to be the eight to ten defining moments in his life, the turning points in his story.

Turning points are defining moments in one's life. They are those times when direction changes—either for good or bad. As Kyle spoke these moments out, we listed them on paper and slowly began to see a mosaic of his life experiences emerging. Life is lived in such a compressed format, with the speed of events, relationships, and other experiences—all formative in their own way—happening far more quickly than we often realize. These turning points bring to the surface the fingerprints of God's shaping hands.

Kyle found himself repeating core themes and patterns in his own development. He would share a significant experience, but then the voice of doubt—questioning if God was really at work. This doubt is common in all of us. It was as if Kyle was—as we often are—afraid to hope. You could hear his cries of hope being crushed each time the wheel of reality went around, and he couldn't see how it all fit together.

When he finished recounting his story, I asked him to summarize what he heard himself sharing. His words were telling:

"Is life as I know it right now all there really is?"

"Is there something more than just living to survive? More than just paying bills?"

"Should I just 'grow up' and accept that this is the best it gets?"

"I've got a new wife. We have a new family. I need to provide for them. Maybe I'm actually being selfish, self-centered, or—even worse—foolish in wanting to believe that there's more!"

"And even if I want to choose a different path, I'm not sure that it would make sense from a practical standpoint."

"It feels as if I'm already trapped by my life circumstances!"

Megan and I watched Kyle as he sifted through both what he had said and how he felt. We could tell that even in words that sounded despairing, something was happening. It was as if he was saying it all out loud to see if he, his wife, and even I would buy it! Would we give in and side with the futility he felt? Or would we challenge him to say what was really on his heart?

Was it "okay" to live his life according to the passion of his heart, or does the logic of his argument keep it from ever being a reality?

Resignation was never the way Kyle had lived up to this point. But he had never really been to such a moment before. Did he buy what the world and culture are offering, or was he willing to truly accept the abundant life Christ offers—even though it required whole-life faith?

After Kyle was finished, we all sat there quietly. Those few seconds felt like eternity. Then, I played a hunch.

"So, Kyle, here's our question thus far: Is this all there is? Is this the best it gets? What do you think?"

And then it happened. After a few minutes of silence, he began to answer my question. As he talked, the insights from deep within his heart began tumbling out onto the table.

"I want—we want—more. Wait, let me say that another way: we believe there is more. We believe that God desires for us to live for more!"

NARRATIVE: THE CALL TO OBEY

We left this time together feeling like a breakthrough was occurring. But we each knew that we weren't there yet. There was more. We later resumed our discussions with Kyle sharing something that proved to be an even more impactful moment than the breakthrough we had just experienced. We jumped right in. He began by sharing what God had been saying to him recently.

Kyle said that more than once over the past few weeks he had clearly heard, in what felt like an audible voice, *Follow me. Kyle, follow me!*

"I still don't know if that is God or just me wanting God to speak to me," he told us. "And even if it is God, where am I supposed to follow to? All I know is that I keep hearing it!"

He continued, "All of this has been going on inside of me, but I don't know what it means—or what to do about it—and I've been a little afraid to share that it's even happening. Honestly, I'm scared of what I might hear back if I actually do answer."

We all just sat in stunned silence for a few minutes.

Typically, I begin these coaching sessions by asking the person to fill me in on what's been happening since our last meeting. But, somehow, this wasn't how Megan or I thought this time would begin. Though it shouldn't be the case, it always is surprising when God moves in and takes over. We who believe constantly need God to help our unbelief.

"Wow!" I blurted out. It was the only profound thing I could think to say.

Tears began to form in each of our eyes.

"And this has been going on now for a week or so? Wow!" I exclaimed again.

We each just sat there with a sense of awe. The Spirit of God was present with us in a palpable way in that moment.

Defining moments are also life-changing moments. Kyle and Megan knew that life would be different from this point forward. It can actually scare many when they finally do see the way God has been at work, as well as where things are leading.

Out of our quietness and tears, it became clear what the new question needed to be. And I knew Kyle really wanted to answer that question, but I also knew it meant leaning into some of his fears. I looked Kyle in the eyes and asked the obvious: "So, what do you think God is asking of you or saying to you? What are you wanting to say back to God, Kyle, as he has called you to follow Him?"

After another long, quiet pause, Kyle sought words to express his thoughts. "I think God is wanting complete control. I think—in fact, I know—that He wants me to follow our hearts and not our heads right now, and make the choices to live our lives differently. To follow him with all of our lives, no matter where it leads—and whatever that means! God is calling me to trust Him and to believe that He can work out all the details and provide for us, even if it means things going differently than we first had planned."

He paused for a minute, but then started again, "I'm not completely sure about this, but I also think God is calling me and Megan deeper into a life of ministry." He said it.

"I think you're exactly right," I affirmed. It was what I also believed, but it was incredibly important for him to hear himself say it and for me to then voice my agreement. Again, what we ourselves discover and bring to the light, we own. What we are told—or what others admit for us—we often still question. In those next moments, I affirmed that God was awakening his heart and inviting him to respond to His calling on his life. I also spent the next few moments affirming that I believed Kyle and Megan were hearing the Lord speak into their lives and that the one true voice, that of the Good Shepherd, was awakening their hearts to His call and shaping work on their lives.

"I don't know where all of this is going," I honestly confessed. "But what I do know is that He is speaking to and leading you both right now. And when he speaks, it's important to respond. God typically unfolds His purposes over time. What's most important is your desire to follow Him, no matter where He leads. That's what is most important and that's what He needs to hear back from you right now. How do you and Megan want to respond to Him in this moment?"

There was little hesitation now in Kyle's response. One of the best things about Kyle's heart for God is that once he sees, he is quick to align.

"Our answer can only be yes!" he said, looking at Megan. "Right?" he voiced as he looked into her eyes. "Absolutely," she said, and they turned toward each other. It was very clear that we were now standing on sacred ground. We all knew it was time to pray.

Kyle started, surrendering the control of his life, their lives, and their future back to God. He poured out his heart to God, giving Him both the right to lead, but also the right to control the future direction of their lives. He confessed his fears related to the provisions needed for their future, as well as confidence for God to provide for them as they grew their family. As Megan joined Kyle in prayer, it was now clear that they were together aligning their hearts with their wills to this new work of God.

For Kyle and Megan, this was a moment similar to when Jesus walked along the shore and spoke with the fishermen. The decision to drop their nets and surrender control and direction over to this person who knew their hearts was a choice that would forever change the direction of their lives and their identity as followers of The Way.

Kyle and Megan had responded similarly. Together, they were surrendering the known and unknown back to God. Instead of following the way most traveled, they were making a break and beginning down a path that believers before them have taken for centuries. What this all meant in terms of the future wasn't clear. But what was clear was that their hearts and their lives would never be the same.

 THE BACK STORY: IDENTITY

Transitions can feel long. They also can feel like God keeps addressing the same issues. What's often occurring is a swinging back and forth between evaluation and alignment.

Looking back at the Transition Life Cycle (page 11), we see arrows depicting this interplay between God bringing perspective and us aligning with His work. It's at this point in a transition that many Christ-followers become impatient. Task-driven and other personality types often fail to wait on the Lord as He works to bring to the surface and address the issues behind the issues. They jettison the progress because of an apparent lack of progress, only to face the same issues again and again somewhere in the future.

New dependency on God needs to be sorted out before He gives to us clarity in how He has shaped us to influence others. Yes, we have gifts, abilities, and even opportunity, but without a new level of dependency, they can be used for our own ruthless ambition. Better men and women than any of us have taken God's call and twisted it to their personal advantage.

CLARIFYING IDENTITY

This is what the LORD says: "Stand at the crossroads and look; ask for the ancient paths, ask where the good way is, and walk in it, and you will find rest for your souls."

—Jeremiah 6:16

Remember your leaders, who spoke the word of God to you. Consider the outcome of their way of life and imitate their faith. Jesus Christ is the same yesterday and today and forever.

—Hebrews 13:7-8

God has been at work shaping each of us for a unique and ultimate contribution. Each moment of our lives, when harvested, provides lessons that shape values and reveal destiny. This way He works is not new. In Hebrews 13, Scripture mandates the study of how God shapes individuals over a lifetime. We are commanded to study His work by examining the lives of those who have gone before us.

During the writing of the book of Hebrews, Jewish followers of Jesus—that is, the first Christians—scattered to distant lands to escape the impending persecution sought to extinguish these claims of Christ being the Messiah. They were exhorted to do three key actions described in Hebrews 13:7-8. Taking these admonishments to heart would help those headed to places unknown, to be faithful to the call on their lives. These same words can also help each of us clarify our identity in Christ. They were told to: (1) remember, to gain important perspective on how they lived their lives; (2), consider, to gain key insights and lessons from their lives; and (3) imitate, to gain new courage to align with how God shapes leaders' lives.

These three mandates serve as three strategic acts for all of us who seek to navigate important, defining moments. History can speak into our history.

- **To remember: Where have you been?** We must gain perspective on how God has shaped His followers in the past.

- **To consider: Where are you going?** We must gain insights related to how His works in the past might inform where He could be leading us in the future.

- **To imitate: Who/what can you do to live it out yourself?** We must gain courage to behave differently, and seek the help of others to stay the course.

These early Christ-followers—like each of us today—were invited to take the ancient path, the "good way" that the Lord continues to use today. The tools of yesterday are the same ones Jesus uses today (Hebrews 13:8). What He used to shape the lives of Moses, Joshua, David, and Isaiah are the same tools He used to shape the Moodys, Wesleys, Calvins, and Wycliffes of church history, as well as the Grahams, Brights, Warrens, and Kellers of our day. God's shaping tools are often the people, events, and circumstances that He brings into our lives. These same tools sculpt and shape each of our lives. Like those early Christ-followers, we too often stand at the crossroads of life with the call to courageously align ourselves with God's shaping work. Regardless of personality type, gender, age, ethnicity, or context, there has been placed within each of us a desire to respond to the One inviting us into a greater plan and story—down a different path.

Taking time to uncover our unique identity in Christ is an important part of our influence for Christ. Leaders know who they are—and who they are not—and they learn how to play their part in the larger story of Christ's Kingdom. Leaders who aren't self-defined are not differentiated, often becoming enmeshed in the organizations and ministries they serve. The message of the Gospel often becomes discredited by Christ-followers who live more for the institution of the Church, than the message and the hope found within living for the one who makes us the Church.

The New Oxford Dictionary defines identity as "the set of characteristics by which a thing is known or recognized. Identity refers to the set of behavioral or personal characteristics by which an individual is recognizable as a member of a group." Personal calling is a summation statement of one's identity as a Christ-follower. It is a holistic summation of one's journey to date, as well as a compass to guide life direction and decision-making. Calling seeks to reflect three major facets of an individual's identity: their unique values, their call to be (biblical purpose), and their call to do (personal vision). Values express the uniqueness of a Christ-follower's journey in a set of core convictions and lessons. Vision and purpose are two sides of the same coin describing the integration of being and doing. Together, these three factors help define one's identity as unfolded by God.

The Awakening Transition sets into motion a series of events, relationships, and circumstances that begin to reveal a sovereign blueprint: the calling of a Christ-follower. Often, for the first time, a Christ-follower begins to catch a glimpse of his or her story in light of Christ's larger narrative. The question is no longer why life should be lived differently, but rather how and what are the choices that will more align and join God in His work.

Passionate Christ-followers and leaders are shaped over a series of life chapters or developmental phases. Each phase moves an individual into greater alignment with God's purposes, as well as an individual's unique and ultimate contribution.

According to J. Robert Clinton in his book *The Making of a Leader*, when we survey the lives of biblical, historical, and contemporary leaders, six generic developmental phases surface:

1. **Sovereign Foundations** (early destiny shaping)
2. **Inner Life Growth** (foundations of spiritual life)
3. **Ministry Maturing** (shaping of calling and contribution)
4. **Life Maturing** (issues of deep processing and identity)

5. **Convergence** (intersection of being and doing)
6. **Afterglow** (reflections and lifelong values and lessons)

The Awakening Transition typically occurs somewhere during the first half of Ministry Maturing, when individuals are challenged on concepts related to gain greater perspective through a series of assignments and experiences. In this transition, a Christ-follower often will begin to seek greater clarity on his or her own life meaning and purpose, as well as issues related to life direction. At its core, understanding life through this lens is to embrace a more developmental paradigm, as opposed to taking a class or completing a workshop. It is anchored in issues of personal discovery and alignment with God's shaping work, as opposed to being a prescribed or generic path forward.

What is your response as you once again face the fork in the road? Will you take the ancient path, the path of alignment and surrender? Will you join Kyle and Megan, who are also choosing to step out of the line and head in a different direction? Or will you succumb to the "new ways"—the ways that seem so fresh and alive and hopeful, only to discover it's merely more of the same?

KYLE'S JOURNAL ENTRY

You realize as you reflect on your journey that certain moments at the time seem fairly insignificant, only to turn out later to be incredibly pivotal and foundational, especially when it comes to God shaping and forming your heart and future. One such instance in my life was the short stint my wife and I spent in Texas. At that time, we had little awareness of the importance of what was taking place around us. It wasn't until we looked back that we saw God's fingerprints all over the place. The deep life-on-life community and mission that we shared with others, as well as the opportunities to lead and grow in ministry, laid the important, early foundations for what God would later build upon.

Along with these moments comes the time of struggle and not knowing what to do with thoughts, feelings, and deep longings that God seems to sovereignly bring to the surface. Moments like these point to new and different stirrings deep inside us. These are also times where God is at work shaping and equipping us for something next, something more. The question, though, is this: what is it?

Having fought my way through years of discontentment in college, only to have the excitement of a new job turn into that same discontentment all over again, things grew increasingly hard to understand. I struggled to keep myself from falling into even deeper discouragement.

I knew in my head that God was still at work shaping me and leading us, but the circumstances playing out did not seem to match up with what I hoped and believed God had in store. Had I foolishly believed the song lyrics that cried, "We were meant to live for so much more?" Had my reading of Scripture that talked about the "good works" God had prepared in advanced for me to do been misunderstood? What do I do with all of this "deep crying out to deep" business that resonates in my soul? What do I do with what seems to be no answer, let alone no way forward? How do I reconcile all of this? Follow Him? Okay, but to where?

So many times in my early life with Jesus, my following was based more on the way that circumstances just seemed to work out. For example, all through college and even after graduating, I never had to apply for jobs. God just gave them to me at the right time, so it was easy to choose, easy to navigate. Up to this point, it was so clear how God's hand was at work in my life, shaping me, leading me.

And yet, knowing God has been at work all along, with far more at stake than ever before, and with more responsibilities hanging over me, it felt as if I couldn't afford to take a step in the wrong direction. I continued to wrestle, wondering if this next leap of faith would play out, or if the cycle of hopeful anticipation would once again lead to more discontentment.

I realized that I had come face-to-face with the nagging issue of trust once again.

As I heard Him speaking, it was easy to doubt at first. But as he continued to faithfully peel back the layers of His plan for me, I began to realize that my hesitations and worries about taking the wrong step and my responsibilities to my wife and family were really my way of staying in control. I had a choice to make—give up or go all in.

Never a quitter, I resolved to go all in. To follow Him.

evaluation and alignment

YOUR JOURNAL ENTRY

Take a moment to write down your thoughts or reactions to this chapter.

THINKING IT OVER

You | One-to-One | Coaching | Group

Below is a guide to help you better process what you've just read. It can be used as you review the ideas personally, as a one-to-one discussion tool, as a small group interaction guide, or as a resource for a coaching conversation between you and a personal development coach.

If you are using *Awakening* with a small group, the following provides reflection questions for your third group conversation.

Reflect on the following quote:

To guide us toward the love that we most desire, we must be taken where we would not go on our own. And lest we sabotage the journey, we must not know where we are going. Deep in the darkness, way beneath our senses, God is instilling "another, better love" and "deeper, more urgent longings" that empower our willingness for all the relinquishment along the way.

—Gerald May, *The Dark Night of the Soul*

Reflect on the following biblical text:

Psalm 20

Reflect on the following questions:

- Where are you in your Awakening Transition?
- What is God causing you to review, realign, or surrender to Him in the process?
- What might be holding you back from full surrender?
- What other times can you recall in your journey that can help you better identify what God might be at work doing right now?

evaluation and alignment

WANT MORE?

Here is a link to Leader Breakthru's Website that will take you further on topics covered in this chapter:

www.leaderbreakthru.com/stuck-the-book

4

direction

He wants to tell us, he has made us to know our reason for being and to be led by it. But it is a secret he will entrust to us only when we ask and then in his own way and his own time. He will whisper it to us not in the made rush and fever of striving and fierce determination to become someone...but rather when we content to rest in him.

—EMILIE GRIFFIN, *CLINGING*

Genuine awakening is the awareness of a door being opened to a whole new dynamic of being. We realize that we have come to a threshold of some sort, and there is need of response. Our response may be immediate, or it may come after much wrestling and recurrence.

—M. ROBERT MULHOLLAND JR., *INVITATION TO A JOURNEY*

THRESHOLD

Kyle had crossed a line. He had entered into the new. He and Megan had surrendered their lives and its direction back to the One who was the author and finisher of their faith (Hebrews 12:2). It was God's call and right to lead their lives. But with all the good that had taken place, the core question still remained unanswered, "What's next?"

Kyle and I sat together again at our favorite local coffee shop. Our coaching time started with me asking him to take a stab at trying to summarize where he and Megan were, and to get me up to speed on what had taken place since our last time together.

"Since our last time," he said. "We feel like we're headed in the right direction. We're both at peace that we've made the right decision and are pretty excited to see how this all will unfold. It feels like that even though we don't know all of what this transition means, whether we should stay with our marketplace careers, or the possibility of some kind of vocational ministry positions, whatever God wants and thinks is the best: that's where we're headed!"

From a young age, Kyle had been around people who had talked about ministry and being "called" into the ministry. It was clear that they meant some kind of church or mission—vocational ministry. Many of those Kyle heard correlated the idea of being "called" to becoming a pastor. The problem was that the "pastor mold" was one that never felt like a good fit for him. His gifts and desires didn't really seem to translate into being an "up front" guy. He led more from the pack. He wanted something different for himself, his generation, and even for the Church. He and Megan hunger for community. He wanted to develop a passionate people, who knew they wanted to live life differently for Christ.

"You know, Kyle, it feels like your transition is readying itself to move now more into the 'direction' phase," I stated. "How all of this will look, where you will end up, and what God has in mind, from our vantage point, it all still feels pretty fluid."

I spent the next few moments trying to explain what might be next in terms of the path of his transition. "When it comes to the final phase of a transition [the direction phase], it's pretty important to remember that we still have a ways to go before things come to an end. But these next few steps won't be boring. In fact, they, could be just the opposite. Get ready for a wild ride that will pick up in terms of options and will require you to stay open, flexible, and moldable. Remember how you gave God control?" I asked. "We need to resist jumping at the first thing and, instead, allow God to bring to you an assignment that matches his shaping. He has designed a next assignment for you both that fits your ongoing development."

Kyle and I also began to actively review the nature and core ideas that surround the Awakening Transition. He was clearly at the point when new direction would mean a series of destiny experiences that would give him pieces of the puzzle that would point the way forward. Together, we reminded ourselves that it would take some time before we made it to the final moments of clarity, but what we wanted was to see these next steps clearly orchestrated and led by God, not Kyle's determination or zeal. Christ was authoring a new focus to his faith and a greater direction for his life.

Things had begun to pick up for Kyle and Megan. Kyle was able to maintain his work with his graphic design company for the time being as he and Megan continued to serve in two different ministries at the church they were attending. They had moved back to their hometown. They were working with young leaders, an emerging passion for both of them. Kyle also loved the chance to do some teaching on Scripture and be involved in leadership training.

At the same time, Kyle was exploring the possibility of doing graphic design work in a freelance capacity, even considering launching his own graphic design company. All was very fluid as he and Megan both decided to back off in terms of a premature decision in order to give God plenty of room to work.

One night after teaching at their church's high school group, Kyle was approached by the senior pastor, who gave him some feedback on his teaching. The pastor also began to explain how he believed God was at work in their church and how important a strong youth ministry was to his vision for the future. Essentially, he shared with Kyle about the possibility of a job opening in the area of youth and college. Kyle knew then that if there was ever something like that opening up he would be interested in exploring what that might actually look like. Over the next few weeks, Kyle and the pastor had several chances to meet and talk, where they shared their hearts, passions for Christ, and their common values. One day, over lunch, an important question surfaced.

DESTINY REVELATION

"So, Kyle," started the pastor, "I was wondering: have you ever really thought about what it would look like for you to come on staff and do ministry at our church?" Though it was something in the back of his mind, Kyle was stunned when the pastor actually asked the question. Though he had thought about the possibility occasionally, it looked to him to be a long way off.

The pastor went on to say, "I think you really have gifts and a potential calling to impact people and I wonder what that would look like for you to use that gifting in a local church." He also went on to express what the future of their church could look like and what might occur if Kyle served as part of the team.

In his past, Kyle had seen both sides of local church ministry: the good and the bad, the rewarding and the challenging. Having grown up in the home of a pastor, he was pretty clear that if he ever headed that direction, it would have to be a clear mandate from God. He was not completely resistant to pastoral ministry as were some, but he didn't see himself in a role of having to carry out all of the duties and responsibilities of pastoral ministry. *Was it really me?* he wondered. *Could it be me, and would the position allow me to be myself?* These and other questions began to invade his thinking. The more they talked, the more Kyle sensed that God was at work, at least enough to give this option some consideration.

At our next coaching time, we had plenty to talk about. And Kyle came ready to process.

"So, I guess you heard, huh?" Kyle began. I smiled as he continued. "I had an interesting lunch this week." His eyes lit up and he pushed his coffee around the table. He was hungry to process all that was going on inside of him. Clearly, he had now seen some of his destiny experiences begin to roll into a potential pathway forward.

"I guess my real question," continued Kyle, "is how all of this fits together. How does this new piece fit together with the sense of calling we've worked on?"

Kyle had worked through core components of the Focused Living Process from Leader Breakthru and had developed clarity related to own personal calling. He pulled out his work and began to give us both his best-understanding-to-date of how he believed God had shaped him for influence, and relating to me his values, his purpose, and some initial thoughts related to his personal vision. I sat and listened as he walked back through his vision.

I asked Kyle to process the potential option of working at the church. His response was now starting to reveal what was really on his heart.

"Up to this point, I've felt that the marketplace might be a better place for me to live out this passion for seeing an authentic faith. I can see myself in various places outside of vocational ministry, reaching out to those who may not fit within the local church. Now, however, I'm wondering if God might me taking this calling He has given me and helping me to see that it can work by being on staff at a local church."

"Keep going," I told Kyle. "These are great questions, and using your calling statement is exactly how to best process a decision like this. Remember earlier when we talked about how your calling is like a compass? It points our lives in a certain direction and provides a true north setting when we evaluate which path we need to take."

"At first glance, if I'm honest, being on staff at a church doesn't seem like an immediate fit, but I also don't want to discard the potential of what God might be doing," Kyle went on. "The pastor does have a vision for seeing transformed lives, reaching neighborhoods, and creating a different, missional culture in the church. That does fit. I think all this is telling me that I need to hear more."

He continued, "It would be good for me to hear more of his vision and how he views my calling fitting into that picture, in light of the needs at the church, and where his vision for the future might take us. I think then I'll be able to determine if what God has put on my heart to be a part of shaping culture matches this church and what it needs. One thing I do know is if the church is looking for more of a traditional youth staff guy, then I am probably not the right fit."

The dramatic awakening and calling of Saul—soon to become Paul—was a call to a corrected view of God and His purposes. The God he said he loved was the God he opposed, blocking how God could work in and through his life. The Awakening Transition we see in Acts 9—and Paul's realignment with the Messiah he had rejected—opened the doors to a new work that earlier was impossible. When God moves, those who follow must be truly willing to follow. This will often mean a change of paradigms, as well as how Christ-followers see both themselves and the purposes of God.

Kyle turned to me, and asked for my thoughts. "So, you've been pretty quiet. What do you think about all of this?"

It was important that he now receive some feedback from my side. We both knew this discussion we were having was critical. "I think you're on it," I stated. "I agree with you that you need more information and that you need to again hear the pastor's heart, especially how his vision lines up with yours. You won't know until you get more time with the one who will be your leader," I said.

"You're right," Kyle responded. "Heart and values have always been important for me, especially if I work on a team with someone and when I know I'm considering a big move like this!"

"Before that time, get together what you have, and let's grab some time and advance the work you've done on your values." I said. "I think it'll be time well-spent and will help you be ready to respond to what might occur during your meeting."

As we worked through each of his values, we teased out in greater detail the actual definitions for each of them and sought to attach and define behaviors that corresponded to each. I could see that Kyle was starting to connect the dots—that things like calling and values were moving beyond abstractions and becoming something that could become part of the decision-making grid that he needed.

"This has been really helpful," Kyle said. "Knowing you, my guess is that you probably want me to flesh out my other values, just like these we worked on, and email them to you. Am I right?" Kyle said with a smirk on his face.

"When do you plan to have them to me?" I responded.

Kyle just smiled.

THE BACK STORY: CALLING

Transitions mark the end of one phase and the beginning of the next. Transitions are the pause in the journey when God consolidates learning and sometimes shifts not only where things are headed, but the paradigms He will use to get us there. Often, what got us to our current place of growth may not be the things that God will use to take us to the next chapter. The beginning of something new often means the closure of something old. One of the core purposes of a transition is to ready a Christ-follower for the challenges ahead.

Some of the emotions attached to these times of closure and change that result from a transition include:

- **Detachment**: Who and what am I really connected to? (Isolation)
- **Displacement**: Where do I belong now? (Loneliness)
- **Dissonance**: What's next? How do I order my day and week? (Confusion)
- **Definition**: Who am I, really? (Identity)
- **Discouragement**: Do I have what it takes? Will this work out? (Doubt)
- **Discernment**: Where am I really going in all of this? (Restlessness)
- **Deepening**: What's the point of all this? (Despair)

In the Awakening Transition, many of these emotions find their way into the process. They're also often some of the ways God uses to bring to the surface life direction and calling. In this period, God stirs the heart—creating a passion for something more—and builds into our life a deeper longing for Him. All of this is tied to finding our place in His greater story.

CALLING

As you continue to watch this transition unfold in Kyle's life, note that the issues he is facing are focused around issues of direction, definition, deepening, and discernment. God is at work reorienting Kyle's compass and life trajectory, aligning him to the true north of God's will and purposes. Awakening is an invitation to bring one's life direction into alignment with the Kingdom path, as opposed to the cultural path. It's about beginning to run a race that God will set before a Christ-follower. It's countercultural. It will run upstream in opposition to living based out of ambition and accumulation. To do this, it will often mean a sense of displacement and loss.

It might sound odd, but often the greatest hurdle for a Christ-follower to embrace God's sovereign call is actually the follower or the church he or she seeks to serve. Preconceived notions related to "professional ministry" have robbed many who are hungry for Kingdom impact. Sometimes, they stumble even before they leave the gate. The clarifying of one's personal calling is an important tool that can help overcomes issues like displacement and isolation.

Paul, Peter, Joshua, and Moses were all summoned. The apostle Paul told King Agrippa that he had been faithful to live out his calling (Acts 21). It's the same summons given to Jeremiah (Jeremiah 3), Esther (Esther 3-4), and many more to follow. It's a call given to both kings and priests.

The clarifying of one's personal calling is a process of dynamic discovery, seeded through one's life experiences and designed to clarify the God-shaped imprint we will each leave on others. The world awaits the impact of men and women who are fully alive—Christ-followers who awaken hearts and even the Church itself.

The Awakening Transition is often a first signal that new life is emerging through the crusty soil of complacency around it. Personal renewal precedes corporate change. In these early days, Christ-followers experience a series of assignments and tasks as the Lord highlights for them values and important core convictions for the days ahead. Vision and direction are often hazy. As calling begins to take shape, what often emerges is a new life. This new life can be surprising to the one experiencing it, but it's one God has intended since the beginning. And one of the keys that this grand design seeks to implant into all of us is a greater recognition of God's voice.

Calling is obviously more than a document. Yet, Christ-followers who can write out their best-understanding-to-date of their personal calling have found that this brief exercise provides the decision-making and directional help they need to navigate the many choices and obstacles along the way.

The process of clarifying one's calling is six-fold and can be found in the Focused Living Process, as well as other tools focused on summarizing God's shaping of a Christ-follower. Steps in the Focused Living Process (available from Leader Breakthru) include:

1. Gaining perspective by creating a personal timeline
2. Developing a list of core values based upon your story so far
3. Developing one's first order call (the call to be)
4. Developing one's second order call (the call to do)
5. Developing a personal calling statement
6. Discerning obstacles that could hold back implementation

Here's how to learn more about the Focused Living Process:
www.leaderbreakthru.com/focused-living

Here's how to access the Focused Living Online Process:
www.leaderbreakthru.com/focused-living-online

PROCESSING

Destiny revelation is often a key tool that God uses to signal the coming together of events and experiences in a Christ-follower's life. Destiny revelation is the moment when a person begins to see and realize the providence of God playing out in his or her future. It's is not something any one can create by his or her own doing—or even something that can be done by others. In retrospect, one can see the hand of God in the life circumstances, timing of events, and contextual factors that press those involved to begin lining up toward God's intended purposes. An accumulation of events that, when viewed together—or at a later point in time—often give confirmation that God is indeed working and signaling a future life direction. Sometimes this kind of activity by God is called the left hand of God.

As a transition begins to move out of the time of evaluation and alignment and into one of direction, destiny experiences are often first on the scene to signal something might be going on. Destiny experiences are one-off occurrences that speak both hope and new potential to the one working through the transition. Up ahead in the direction phase of the transition is the idea of destiny fulfillment: the time when the events have orchestrated themselves to the point of decision and acceptance of the new direction. It also signals the beginning of the end of a transition.

KYLE'S JOURNAL ENTRY

As I worked my way through this transition, I intuitively knew that it was important for me to be sensitive to my own heart and true motives. Time and time again, I asked myself the hard questions: Why do I want this? Is it because this is what I've known and seen throughout my life? I remember praying and asking God to reveal to me any impure motives that were buried deep in my heart. I was desperate to know that the steps I was taking were in direct response to where God was already at work in me, and not just me jumping at the first good opportunity to come my way.

My heart has always been one of my greatest assets. Aware of this, I continued to ask myself questions like: Am I doing this because it feels easier? Because it seems attractive? Do I just want the attention that comes from leadership? Do I like how others might perceive me as being "significant" because of the "prestige" this position offers?

Above all else, I needed to know that I was doing this not because I was following my earthly father who is in vocational ministry, but because I was wholly surrendered to my Father in heaven, following Him wherever He might lead. Before I was ready to respond to the new and exciting opportunity in front of me, I had to first make sure that this was actually God. I had already jumped once—in my mind, this next leap needed to be the right one, otherwise I knew my heart would still be unsettled and left longing. I needed God to search my heart, so I prayed much like King David does in Psalm 51. I knew I needed to take time to listen to God and not just do all of the talking.

I also needed to remind myself—and be okay with the fact—that God's answer to this new opportunity could very well be "no." As hard as it was, I had to open myself up for God to examine me, and regardless of the outcome trust that He would be faithful to complete the work He had started. The process left me feeling completely exposed, like an acrobat in mid-air who finds out his safety net has been removed. Even in the midst of my vulnerability, it still felt right—I still felt safe. And God continued to show himself faithful as I chose to trust Him.

awakening

YOUR JOURNAL ENTRY

Take a moment to write down your thoughts or reactions to this chapter.

THINKING IT OVER

You | One-to-One | Coaching | Group

Below is a guide to help you better process what you've just read. It can be used as you review the ideas personally, as a one-to-one discussion tool, as a small group interaction guide, or as a resource for a coaching conversation between you and a personal development coach.

If you are using *Awakening* with a small group, the following provides reflection questions for your fourth group conversation.

Reflect on the following quote:

> *I am a pilgrim, but my pilgrimage has been wandering and unmarked… Often my fairest hopes have rested on bad mistakes as I cross a dark valley. And yet—for a long time looking back, I have been unable to shake off the feeling that I have been led all along—make of that what you will.*
>
> —Wendell Berry, *Jaber Crow*

Reflect on the following biblical text:

Psalm 77

Reflect on the following questions:

- Talk about the "almost" moments of your life—those times when you "almost" made a choice, did something else, or went to a certain place, but did not. What did you learn from these moments?

- What are the pros and cons of the term "destiny" for you? Do you believe your life has a sense of destiny?

- If God were to move in and give you one answer or reassurance right now in terms of the work He is doing in your life, what would you like to hear?

WANT MORE?

Here is a link to Leader Breakthru's Website that will take you further on topics covered in this chapter:

www.leaderbreakthru.com/awakening/calling

5
challenge

When we were given the capacity to love, to speak, to decide, to dream, to hope and create and suffer, we were also given the longing to be known by the One who wants to be completely known.

—ROBERT BENSON, *BETWEEN THE DREAMING AND THE COMING TRUE*

We may ignore, but we can nowhere evade the presence of God. The world is crowded with Him. He walks everywhere incognito. And the incognito is not always hard to penetrate. The real labor is to attend. In fact, to come awake. Still more, to remain awake.

—C.S. LEWIS

DECISION

Kyle came and sat down next to me in the pew before the worship service started. I could tell that he had things swirling around inside—ideas, possibilities, pitfalls, and challenges. Making the right decision is no easy task, especially when you know what you decide will take you down new paths.

"Any chance of getting some time soon?" he asked. He had just completed the interview process with the church.

"Sure!" I responded. "How about tomorrow?"

Kyle had taken all the right and steps. He had asked those who knew him best and had sought their counsel. He had invested time in the Word and sought to discern its guidance. He had been active in his journaling. He and Megan had spent some key time in prayer. They had both consulted and asked for input from parents, family, and friends. But decision time was here.

The church was considering its logistics. Things related to the budget were being worked through. At this point, things seem quiet, but the ball rested in Kyle's court. It was a good time for another coaching conversation.

"I've really wanted to do this whole thing right," Kyle admitted. "This is big!" He continued, "The funny thing is that now we're getting close to making a decision and things are feeling pretty right, but, for some reason, things seem quiet on God's side of things. It almost feels like He's waiting on me. Weird! I wanted it to be so much faster, but I guess now that I'm at the deciding point, it feels like I need things to slow down. Is this normal?"

I smiled and responded, "You've done a great job trying to process all this. I think you probably already have a pretty good idea that it's time to make a call and decide if this is what God wants! So it's not surprising that it brings on some nerves. Every time I have had to make a call like this, I've felt the very same things."

Kyle nodded, appreciating the encouragement, but was really in need of some assurance. I spent a few minutes making sure we were both on the same track: that Kyle would get what he needed out of this conversation and that he was ready for my input. It was important.

Kyle went first.

"I think I have enough information, have asked enough people I respect, and it feels like I have a pretty good handle on what's being offered and what I really want to do. I guess the question is really whether going on staff at a church is the right fit for me."

"I really like the pastor and believe in him, but how committed is the rest of the church to what he envisions, especially adopting a more missional focus? Is the church really willing to make some of the tough decisions to head in a new direction?"

"Did you get any of that answered when you talked earlier with the pastor?" I asked. "After you came back from that first round of discussion with him, you felt like they really wanted you to come on staff not just to help fill some needs, but also to be part of helping to chart a new direction for the church, right? Was there more than that you're needing or wanting to hear?"

"I guess," Kyle shared, "I'm still wondering, though, if this is a place that will allow me to be myself. I know I need a place to be trained and developed—and I'm new at all of this—but I also know I need to be faithful to this call I believe God has entrusted to Megan and myself."

"Absolutely! I agree" I responded. "That's what this is all about. Clarifying God's call on your lives." We were at a key moment in his long transition. Kyle was fighting for the chance to be who God had called him to be. This moment was worthy of the struggle and effort.

"One thing I know about you, Kyle," I started, "is that if you commit, you're all the way in! It's one of the best things about you. To me, it sounds like you need to make sure that everything you're feeling lines up." Kyle paused and then spoke, "If I'm going to be a passionate supporter of a different kind of church, I think I need to hear one last time about the values driving this pastor to lead this church in this direction, and that I that I feel right about having his back!"

Ahead of Kyle was the most the important choice and decision of his newfound calling. There are important moments like these when choices need to be made and when Christ-followers feel most vulnerable. I know who I am, but if I chose this course, will I really get the chance to be me?

"What are you thinking, Kyle?" I asked.

"I think it would be really good for me to get one final time in with the pastor," he replied, "just to make sure that my heart and passion to engage culture, build community, and develop people are critical parts of his vision for the church in the future."

"Yep," I responded. "Good call. I also think that God may have gone quiet right now to see if you'll just 'accept the job' or if you'll you use what He has taught you [values] and the way He has created you [identity] to help make this decision."

Kyle could sense that we'd come to a point of agreement on what his next steps needed to be. "If I go to the pastor, I need to talk to him on a heart level and trust that my core passions will either connect on not connect with him on that level."

"Exactly!" I replied.

We both sat quietly, trying to sort through all that we'd just discussed.

"If you're open, can I give you one additional thought?" I asked.

"Sure!" he responded.

"When I coach people in the Awakening Transition, it's different than when I'm coaching someone facing the Deciding Transition, which typically takes places in a person's 50s or 60s. What I'm trying to say here is that what you're facing won't be forever. This is the first of several potential assignments that lie ahead in your life with God."

I continued, "I believe God has built into this time of transition the purpose of you being able to go deeper in your capacity to hear God's voice, trust what He is saying to you deep within, and follow Him wholeheartedly. This assignment and staff position may or may not work out for the long haul. I hope it works. Regardless, its outcome will mean a greater capacity to follow God and to know when He is speaking to you about who He has shaped you to be and how He is developing you as a leader."

I often watch those I coach focus so hard on the decision at hand that they miss out on the real purpose of what God is intending to do in them through a transition. It's important to get all you can out of your transitions. Sometimes that means the decision at hand is second to the deeper work of how God wants to form your character.

"True," Kyle replied. "God is sometimes doing more than whether or not I get everything right. In the end, how I do this is as important as what I do. And if I do my best to discern what He is doing and wanting me to do, God will take care of me—and us."

"Yes!" I acknowledged. "God is the one responsible for your development. How He does it and pulls it all off I haven't got a clue! But what I can tell you that if you and I are surrendered to His purposes, He causes all things to work together for good (Romans 8:28). Sometimes, we know what He is doing, but often He's using circumstances like these to teach us more than what is apparent."

We both sat there for a few minutes and began to realize that we had gone just about as far as we could go for this coaching conversation. "So, what do you see to be your next steps, Kyle?" I asked.

"Well, I think I need to set up that appointment with the pastor. Then it's time for Megan and I to go before the Lord to make our decision."

"Sounds good to me," I said. "What was most helpful for you during our time together today?" I asked.

"I think when we were able to boil it all down to needing to follow my instincts and make this decision from my heart. That really helped. When my heart is at peace, then I know I can be all in and just let things unfold." He looked relieved.

"How about I pray for this next meeting with the pastor?" I said.

Kyle and I spent the next few moments in prayer, asking the Lord make Himself present in this situation in order to show Kyle what He was at work doing and to give him the capacity to clearly hear God's voice as he met with the pastor.

Somewhere, probably not more than a few miles from where you are reading this book right now, it's very possible that a coach and a young Christ-follower have just bowed their heads to ask God for guidance, just like Kyle and I did that day. It happens each day, all around the globe.

FAITH CHALLENGE

It was late in the afternoon when I got the call. I remember it pretty clearly because I'd been waiting and praying for most of the day. It's not always easy to be the coach. I've found it's much harder to walk alongside and leave the results up to God.

But ownership and empowering others to decide means everything when it comes to Kingdom expansion. It's about teaching them to fish versus just getting them some fish from the grocery store. There's a much greater likelihood that transformation will occur when you create moments of discovery, as opposed to solving everyone's problems for them.

Finally, the phone buzzed in my pocket. "Hey, its me!" said an upbeat Kyle. "Thought I'd give you a quick update on how it went!"

"Great," I said. "I was hoping it was you! How'd it go?"

"Well, it went better than I expected. And after hearing the pastor's heart and walking back through his vision one more time, I felt God prompt me to communicate that I'm in! Megan and I had prayed before and agreed that if it went like we hoped, I would say yes! So, it looks like if all the final paperwork goes through, I'll be the new high school and college pastor at the church."

"Outstanding, bud!" I exclaimed. "I can hear the excitement in your voice!"

"Yeah, and probably also a lot of relief," Kyle said, sighing. "I'm glad to finally know how this is going to play out, and I feel good about what we did in order to get here. I also know I couldn't have gotten here without your help! I just wanted to say thanks!"

"You're welcome," I replied. "From my side, this really feels right and I'm proud of the way you've processed all of this! It hasn't been easy."

Kyle had now entered the final stage of a transition: the Direction Phase of the Transition Life Cycle. "By the way," said Kyle. "You know that transition diagram you keep showing me?" he asked. "Am I close to the end of all this? I don't think I can take much more!"

"No. I'm thinking you're near the end of the transition!" I happily reported. "In fact, my guess is that we just moved into the Direction Phase with the acceptance of the position. In personal development language, we call that moment 'destiny fulfillment.'" I went on to explain that "destiny fulfillment" is when direction moves to closure of a transition.

"I like the sound of that!" said Kyle.

"But there's one more thing we need to talk about," I stated. "Sometimes, the only thing worse than not doing what God wants each of us to do is knowing what He wants you to do!"

"Keep going," said Kyle.

"At the end of every transition, there's typically something called a Faith Challenge," I offered. "Though it's now clear what God has been unfolding, this new chapter will require a real step of faith! As you close one door, it takes faith to walk through another," I continued. "My guess is that ahead of you is a hard conversation with the company that gave you your start. I know how loyal you are. It could be a tough to go in and tell them of your decision, even if it's right!"

"And along with that," I went on, "you're cutting the strings of that financial provision and now placing your family clearly into God's hands as you head down the path of vocational ministry."

"Yeah. Been thinking about that," said Kyle. "It'll be hard to have that conversation. I really appreciate all they did for me! And I definitely do take a pay cut to move in this direction."

"You know," Kyle reflected. "I've sometimes wondered how I might respond if I ever came to this moment in my life. I watched you and Mom cope with all of this. And now it looks like it's my turn."

I could tell that this was the right move for Kyle to make, even though it also was a hard thing. Good things can also be hard things.

"A Faith Challenge is a time when God calls us to put weight down on what we believe He has revealed," I explained. "Faith challenges are very much a part of a transition, as God calls us to move beyond all that we know in order to be able to move into the new and unknown. We spent the final minutes of our time together just talking through what life might look like in the days ahead.

"So, any assignments, coach?" Kyle asked.

"Not really!" I said. "We're at that point where what's ahead is living it out, and behaving your way into the future!"

My final words actually served to put a capstone on our time together.

"You were made for all of this, Kyle," I stated. "The reason I believe all of this will work is because it is God who has been at work throughout it all. Our hope is that He who began this work will continue to be at work in the days to come [Philippians 1:6]. I'm excited for you, Kyle!"

He closed us in prayer.

 THE BACK STORY: TWO TRACKS

"And David shepherded them with integrity of heart; with skillful hands he led them."

—Psalm 78:72

Living as a Christ-follower is the interplay of doing and being. Skilled hands must be guided from hearts shaped to live with integrity. These are the twin pillars of godly influence. God shapes us through a process of dual formation: what we do and who we are. Being and doing.

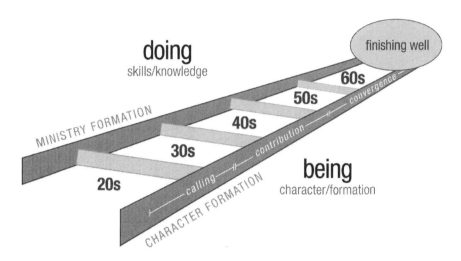

A children's song, sung by many American churches over the last 40 or so years, provides a tip to discovering of one's call and the awakening of one's passion:

> *Deep and wide.*
> *Deep and wide.*
> *There's a fountain flowing deep and wide.*
> *Deep and wide.*
> *Deep and wide.*
> *There's a fountain flowing deep and wide.*

In Mark 3:13-15, Jesus signals to the early disciples—and to us, as well—how someone with an awakened heart was to live and minister: "He climbed a mountain and invited those he wanted with him. They climbed together. He settled on twelve, and designated them apostles. The plan was that they would be with him, and he would send them out to proclaim the Word and give them authority to banish demons" (*The Message*).

Note the order here:

1. he "invited those he wanted with him"
2. "that they would be with him"
3. that "he would send them out to proclaim the Word"
4. "and give them authority to banish demons"

This, then, is how it works: one's authority to minister is the result of regular times of intimacy and a deepening of one's relationship with God. Put simply: don't not try to minister for God without investing in time to be with God.

The breadth of each of our impact and ministry is tied to the depth of our intimacy with Christ. This is the clarion message of the Awakening Transition and the pattern for success. Many have tried to void or skip this step, but Christ was clear: the call to follow me is a call to be with me, even—and especially!—before you try to go out and do great things for me. There are no shortcuts. This is "the" pattern. It's one that both awakens a heart to God and causes it to hear at life's end, "Well done, good and faithful servant!" (Matthew 25:21).

God gives Christ-followers many assignments (Ministry Formation), but really only one core priority: to love God with all our heart, mind, body, and soul. Through that corridor, will we be able to love our neighbors as ourselves and discover the "good works" for our lives that the Triune God authored before time began. To the awakened soul, these first assignments help create both power and the edge to make an impact.

There are many temptations to do things differently. That's why it all comes down to trust and obedience. Trust is about relationship. Fruit that remains comes from the process of learning to abide in Christ (John 15). Many baby boomers now confess that the church they leave behind is "a mile wide and an inch deep." If ministry is to truly be of Christ, then it can only come out of the early pattern that Jesus set for his disciples—a pattern that cannot be avoided by those who have followed since those early days. Intimacy with Christ always precedes authority given by Christ.

Ministry formation refers to the tasks, assignments, challenges, and opportunities that come into a Christ-follower's life to shape his or her life and ministry. Typically, in the Awakening Transition, some of the fresh, new thinking and expressions are birthed by those who are young and stand outside the norm, seeking to speak into the Church the need for new skills and greater abilities. Without these, the Church ceases to witness to the Gospel in fresh ways. But ministry formation void of character formation can provide a spiritual mask for personal ambition and cravenness.

Character formation is the cultivation of the inner life. It's about interior growth and one's personal walk with Christ. It's about shaping the heart and softening attitudes. It's about filling the well, the ongoing process of redemption and sanctification, and the call to being the holy priesthood, set apart to do good works. Character formation is about the Potter's hands that mold and shape a life to recognize and respond to the work and works of God.

Together, the two tracks of being and doing—both occurring simultaneously in their impact—create a spark that ignites a different kind of follower and lives so changed that God uses him or her to be part of changing others. The only thing that matters is changed lives: lives awakened to the life and call of God. Once hearts are awakened, then the journey begins toward a unique and ultimate contribution for the King.

 THE AWAKENING TRANSITION: SUMMARY

All transitions are unique, but all transitions carry with them the fingerprints of our God. When you evaluate the development of many Christ-followers over time, you begin to see a generic path. One of the distinguishing traits of a transition is that they rarely stick to a single event. Instead, they unfold over time, often taking between three months and three years. Transitions are like mini journeys and typically take place in four parts: (1) entry, (2) evaluation, (3) alignment, and (4) direction.

The Awakening Transition that we've just discussed above is one typically experienced by those in their 20s or 30s and is used by God to clarify issues of life direction, identity, and calling. Let's walk our way back through Kyle's transition.

1. It Begins: Entry Phase

Typically, transitions don't quickly identify themselves. It was clear that something was occurring with Kyle, but it was unclear what God was doing, as well as when Kyle's transition actually began. The uncertainty and restlessness was our sign, yet he was initially afraid to believe that it was more than just frustration over his job.

Entry into a transition typically occurs much earlier than one thinks. Often, we're well into a transition before we recognize what is occurring. Walking with the help of someone alongside us (like a coach or mentor) can help process the reality of a transition. Kyle was so busy trying to understand where he was and what his disillusionment was with the job he had always wanted that it was hard for him to acknowledge the reality of his transition. His ongoing frustration with his circumstances and his growing hunger for something more and/or different is common for those who have entered a transition.

Entry time of a transition often shows itself as a period of questions, not answers, especially with those facing the Awakening Transition. Issues related to life direction and calling have often been occurring and other solutions have often been tried before coming to terms with the fact that what was occurring is not going away.

As I listened to Kyle in those early days, I could almost hear a heart that was afraid to beat. His early step with taking the job made him hesitant to step out again. Too many times, God's stirring gets trampled by the facts and obstacles that come with life. They can also go unrecognized, unlabeled, and even undervalued in the life of Christ-followers, especially in the hearts of the young. These Christ-followers begin to believe that their time will never come and that if they wanted to follow their heart, it will come down to issues of a paycheck and things like school bills.

2. It Unfolds: Evaluation Phase

As Kyle settled into the reality that something was occurring and his frustration now had a name and even a purpose, the process of reviewing what was actually occurring in his transition began. It took time for new insights to emerge, but as he dealt with issues of trust and control, you could begin to see that he became more at peace that God was at work.

God then began to speak in greater ways.

As his coach, it was very tempting to suggest answers and give solutions way ahead of when he was ready for them. Kyle and I both, together, needed to go on this journey that would take time. As I continued to listen, I was also trying to discern the questions related to his heart. A big part of who he is has to do with him being able to trust the instincts and discernment God has given to him. I had to keep throwing the processing back to him before I shared. My role was to keep listening and to keep asking him questions to help him process what he was feeling. In coaching, this is known as coaching on the "Third Level," where he and I have actually joined the one being coached and together we are assessing his options together. (For more on "Third Level" coaching, check out *Co-Active Coaching: Changing Business, Transforming Lives* by Henry Himsey-House, Karen Kimsey-House, Phillip Sandahl, and Laura Whitworth.)

The Evaluation Phase of a transition is often a time when God brings greater self-awareness to the person being coached. Most people aren't very self-aware and they often assume that what they experience is what all people experience. Kyle grew in his acceptance that Christ had shaped his heart and had woven a set of core values into his life and development. The further we went into the transition, the more I saw Him able to show Kyle more of Himself, and give him handles on how to recognize His shaping work.

When Christ-followers grow in their self-awareness, they also typically increase in hope that God is at work in their lives. And the more they hope, the more courage comes to the surface, as well as a willingness to follow God to new places. The Evaluation Phase takes time. To short-circuit the process means to short-circuit the growth.

3. Time to Decide: Alignment Phase

I remember watching the moment when Kyle began letting go of some of the reasons and obstacles that were holding him back from considering vocational ministry. Doubt and fear are part of all of us. For God to do a new work, He often must bring to the surface the roadblocks and obstacles that keep us from seeing the next stage of development emerge.

The acknowledgement of Kyle's resistance to taking a staff position in a local church because of what he sees in the current expressions of church life was an important piece in what God was doing. The exercise he went through to help him clarify his values and calling needed to play an important role in his decision-making process. God used this exercise to confront the deeper issues related to trust, and the need to listen to his heart. Kyle's struggle, as with many young leaders today, with the institutional Church was very much a real issue. But the deeper issue was tied to what God was calling him to do.

Kyle's meetings with the pastor were the turning points in the transition and signal the crossover between the Alignment Phase—Kyle's willingness to surrender to God's deeper work—and the Direction Phase of the transition. Though the job offer felt like it came out of the blue, as you look back, you can see how God had been positioning Kyle for that moment. Kyle and Megan's experiences in Texas and ministry opportunities for Kyle to work with the youth and teach all signaled a growing passion to influence others, his heart for people, his hope for church to be done in fresh ways, and his desire to be part of a local church that was making a difference.

4. The End: Direction Phase

As Kyle reached the end of his transition, things rapidly began to fall in place as the Lord began to connect the dots. Does it always happen this way? Certainly not. But it does sometimes. Direction does involve a series of destiny experiences. Whatever is ahead, it will always involve a Faith Challenge moment when Christ-followers must put new trust in the God they are called to follow. Kyle's new family and their needs were—and still are today—very real and important concerns. But his greatest battle in all of this was wanting to believe and trust, though some obstacles helped at times to fuel his unbelief.

One reason I knew God had placed me in the position of being Kyle's coach was that I've faced some of Kyle's same battles. In my past, I had quietly vowed that I would never put myself and my family in a position where we would live based on the faith giving of others. So, when God began to lead my wife and I into pastoral ministry, there were some struggles and doubts. But then when He pushed us farther, calling us into missionary-type positions and the raising of our own support, my doubts turned into major obstacles.

"Lord, I can't put my family through that! You know it'll be too hard for Robin!"

Translation: "Lord, I don't trust you to bring in what we need. I don't believe you can or will provide!"

In that moment, I was hiding my own lack of trust behind my family. I too needed to come face-to-face with my lack of trust that where God guides, He provides. I needed to come to the end of me, in order to find a new dependency on Christ. More than 22 years later, Robin and I look back and see clear evidence of God's provision from those who chose to trust in Christ, over and over again. It will always come down to—as well as come back to—the issue of trust.

The end of Kyle's transition, like all transitions, meant a Faith Challenge, a processing item God uses to advance our understanding of His character and ability to lead our lives.

Stepping away from a steady paycheck and allowing his family to go "off road" into uncharted terrain was a big step. Kyle needed to know for certain that God had authored this next step in his journey.

What Kyle takes with him from this transition are many lessons about the character of God and the new level of trust that following Christ requires. All transitions help to consolidate core values and lessons. These become anchor points and guiderails for the future. At its core, Kyle's Awakening Transition was about not running ahead or letting impatience and frustration with life take him off the path. In new ways, Kyle has now learned to follow Christ and to let Him be the one to set the course. New challenges will certainly come and God is not done by any means in His shaping of Kyle and Megan. But, for now, their hearts are awakened to His call on their lives. The days ahead will never be the same.

KYLE'S JOURNAL ENTRY

As I look back on the completion of my own Awakening Transition, I wish I could say I do so in fondness and with a sense of reminiscing. But, truthfully, it was a very difficult and challenging season of my life. More times than I can count, I resigned myself to throwing in the towel, believing for a moment that whatever misery and discontentment that first catapulted me into this transition had to have been better than the all of the growing pains I was experiencing as I learned to trust God's leading and voice through uncharted territory. But each time I picked up the proverbial towel, God was quick to remind me of His plans to give me a hope and a future. If He had ever been at work in my life, He was still at work.

The good news about this season of awakening and transition is just that: it's a season. It has a beginning. And it has an end.
Jeremiah 29:11 is one of those feel-good verses that's easy to grab onto during a time of transition. How good it is to know that God has a plan for us! Not a plan to harm or destroy us, but a plan to give us hope and a future! Heck, that's why they put that verse on coffee mugs and calendars! But, in my time of transition, I found the true power of that verse to be in the setup (verses 4-10).

Much like the Israelites who were in captivity, my time of transition was often a painful reminder that I was not "home"—that I was not in a land or a place where I wanted to be. I felt uprooted, overlooked, and heartsick for something more. Yet, in the midst of what felt like exile from the desires of my heart, God was inviting me to listen to His voice and trust him. His loving exhortation to me was to stop fighting the fact that I was not "home" and to start sinking my roots deep down in to what He was at work doing in me.

The invitation before me in my time of transition was to press in. To get everything I could out of this season. To learn what it meant to be fully surrendered. To know and to trust that still, small voice as it steadily and lovingly directs and guides. God was inviting me to make my home in the transition for however long it would last—for He knew the plans He had for me, plans that gave great hope and a more beautiful future than anything I could imagine.

From where I sit today, on the other side of the Awakening Transition, I can tell you that not everything is roses and lilies. Doubt creeps in from time to time, and questions as to whether or not I'm in the "right" place surface here and there. But, in the midst of it all, I'm reminded that the same God who was so faithful to stir all of this up in me in the first place will continue to be faithful as He gently continues His refining and shaping work in me, His beloved son.

challenge

YOUR JOURNAL ENTRY

Take a moment to write down your thoughts or reactions to this chapter.

THINKING IT OVER

You | One-to-One | Coaching | Group

Below is a guide to help you better process what you've just read. It can be used as you review the ideas personally, as a one-to-one discussion tool, as a small group interaction guide, or as a resource for a coaching conversation between you and a personal development coach.

If you are using *Awakening* with a small group, the following provides reflection questions for your fifth group conversation.

Reflect on the following quote:

> *He leads us step-by-step, from event to event. Only afterwards, as we look back over the way we have come and reconsider certain important moments in our lives in the light of all that has followed them, or when we survey the whole progress of our lives, do we experience the feeling of having been led without know it, the feeling that God has been mysteriously guiding our lives, all along.*
>
> —Paul Tournier, *The Adventure of Living*

Reflect on the following biblical text:

Psalm 25

Reflect on the following questions:

- Talk about the decision-making process Kyle used. What were the strengths of how he came to the point of decision? Weaknesses? How is it similar or different than the process you typically use?
- What would have been to be some of the emotions you would have experienced if you were in Kyle's shoes?
- The Direction Phase isn't just about moving forward; it's also about a Faith Challenge. What are the issues you face—or will face—that will challenge you the most as you move beyond the Awakening Transition?

WANT MORE?

Here is a link to Leader Breakthru's Website that will take you further on topics covered in this chapter:

www.leaderbreakthru.com/ten-ways-god-builds-character

6

postures

WAYS TO RESPOND TO THE AWAKENING TRANSITION

What deadens us most to God's presence within us, I think, is the inner dialogue that we are continuously engaged in with ourselves, the endless chatter of human thought. I suspect that there is nothing more crucial to true spiritual peace...than being able from time to time to stop that chatter, including even the chatter of spoken prayer.

—FREDERICK BUECHNER, *TELLING SECRETS*

(Kyle Walling)

Discipline is defined as "training expected to produce a specific character or pattern of behavior" (New Oxford Dictionary). Discipline is a natural component of the Christian life. In fact, almost nothing of any significance in our lives is ever accomplished without it.

Spiritual disciplines help to move us deeper into the heart of God and produce Christ-like characteristics and behavior in our lives. Disciplines of engagement and restraint may change over time based on the seasons and stages in a leader's development, but there are a few core postures that are important to practice and can help greatly with navigating the Awakening Transition. Embracing and practicing these disciplines isn't some magic formula, but doing so can help to posture your heart in a way that allows you to gain the most from this time of transition.

Leadership Emergence Theory is a field of study that seeks to identify principles that reflect how God shapes his followers over his or her lifetime. This body of research, undertaken by J. Robert Clinton, has informed and guided the development of leaders during all three of the transitions and provides insights into the essential choices and disciplines that help leaders to finish well.

The following three practices and/or disciplines emerged from both the research and coaching of leaders that help facilitate navigation of the Awakening Transition: (1) listening, (2) chronicling, and (3) leaning.

LISTENING

All Christ-followers who finish the race well commit themselves to growing in their ability to recognize the voice of God over the course of their lifetimes. The farther one goes, the greater the need to listen, recognize, and embrace that still, small voice. Those who finish well live intentionally, choosing to see and live from God's sovereign perspective. They are regularly able to disengage from the urgent circumstances around them and move to the higher ground in order to see the greater narrative being worked out in their lives. They fight back in terms of the numbing grind that comes at times with the endless days, weeks, and months of looking at the same. They break the mundane with purpose, intentional behavior, and new rhythms.

Many good tools exist to help provide this perspective. Yet, what matters most is not a preoccupation with the perfect tools, app, book, or method, but that you as a Christ-follower find what works best for you. Transitions point to the need for new ways to listen and better recognize what God is at work doing.

Here's one simple approach that can create listening space. The discipline and posture of listening is not natural for most of us. Through schooling, we have been encouraged to take "speech" classes, not "listening" classes. The more we practice this posture of listening, the more we see Kingdom results produced in our lives. When should we be sure to practice the discipline of listening? Every day, every week, every month, every quarter, and every year.

For listening to produce greater voice recognition of the King—as opposed to wondering whose voice is speaking—it requires a rhythm that is practiced regularly. Here's a simple guide as you begin to practice this disciple and listen your way through this transition:

- **Every Day**: 20-30 minutes reflecting on my week and key issues

- **Every Week**: 2-3 hours where I bust free and reflect

- **Every Month**: 1 day away, when no one—but my spouse, of course!—can find me

- **Every Quarter**: 1 overnight so that I can totally disconnect

- **Every Year**: 2-3 days when I review the past and plan for what is ahead

The discipline of listening often also exposes the need to be more proactive in our planning ahead. By planning ahead and even scheduling listening into your daily, weekly, monthly, quarterly, and yearly calendars, you'll be better able to find the space to break from the urgent and effectively practice this discipline. Typically, it's best to plan a quarter ahead. It also often requires communicating with others who will be most impacted by you setting up regular times for you and God.

It will be a dogfight to not let the tyranny of the urgent overcome the call for greater discipline. Turning down the roar and the noise of our day is often the biggest challenge related to godly perspective.

Here are four ways to help facilitate your listening:

1. Find a regular spot and declare it to be your place of sanctuary. Make it so that every time you go by it in a day, it reminds you as the place where you go to listen to and be with God.

2. Disconnect from being connected. Cell phone off (not just on silent). Stop texting. Don't take calls or check your email. This is a time of solitude and rest.

3. Instead of going big and long right away, grace yourself to first take 10 minutes of quiet, allowing yourself time to do nothing, solve nothing, and just rest in God's presence. The more you practice listening, the more you can extend out the time.

4. Once you complete your listening, spend a few minutes to journal down what you found yourself thinking about and/or what you felt like God was saying to you.

Resist making this a time in which you pressure yourself to have to "accomplish something." Instead, allow it to be a time when you quit talking to God and you offer up to Him the worship of listening to Him.

CHRONICLING

To "chronicle" is to record important or historical events as they transpire in their order of occurrence. Chronicling also includes the adding of commentary and additional information so that one can return to events in order to draw insights from them. This is why I've chosen to use the word "chronicling" as opposed to "journaling."

Intentional and regular documenting of one's journey as a Christ-follower is about more than just the recording of events as they occur. Instead, it's a catalog of emotions, feelings, truths, and doubts as you walk the sometimes lonely and nebulous path of Christian life and leadership. Chronicling transforms journaling into a tool that, over time, can offer great perspective, becoming a personal development map that a follower can look back on as they desire insights for the future.

Although rich with meaning, the term "chronicling" itself can easily be construed as a non-personal or overly detailed and demanding discipline that it moves out of the realm of what feels comfortable and authentic. Chronicling is something that can and should be done as you go—making notes and writing down big questions and future dreams as they surface. The challenge is to go one step beyond recording your prayers, feelings, and dialogue with your thoughts, and to begin to record and reflect on what is occurring around you as God works, documenting the important moments of your journey each day.

I remember seeing the journals of one of my close friends with whom I have partnered in ministry. I noticed how they were arranged with the year scribed on the outside spine, each lined up next to the others on his shelf. At that time, I was in a place of not really knowing how to really journal and was an infrequent "journaler" at best. One of my first responses to his discipline in journaling his prayers, heart, and thoughts was one of pure intimidation and inadequacy—wondering if I would ever be able to do something like that. But, when I told him what I felt, his response was to try to minimize the wound I was inflicting on myself due to my lack of discipline. "Kyle, this is where I do all of my thinking, where I take notes about what I see God doing each day. It's where I'm actively chronicling and processing everything related to ministry and my own heart. For me, I need it all in once place. Besides, it has taken me time to develop my way of doing this—it didn't just happen overnight!"

With my friend's encouragement, I began to do the same. Tucked in a drawer at our house are three black journals with the dates of the corresponding years. Though the process of chronicling has become much more natural and fluid over time, it still requires a measure of effort, intentionality, and discipline to keep it going. Flipping through the pages, one would quickly find gaps of several weeks and even months where I have allowed other things to take precedence over my time reflecting and recording. Chronicling and journaling are priceless disciplines that offer perspective for one's entire journey, but become essential as one looks to process transitions and discern what God is actively at work doing in one's life.

Here are four questions that can help you as you seek to "chronicle" your thoughts, hopes, dreams, questions, frustrations, failures, and journey with God:

1. **What's right?** Write about those things in your life that you feel are right and that you sense are in line with truth, honesty, an openness to God, and God's ongoing refinement of your life.

2. **What's wrong?** Write about what you know is not right, and what the Spirit has brought to the surface or patterns that you see that take away from God and His purposes.

3. **What's missing?** Write about those things that you are realizing are not a part of the rhythm of your daily life, activities, or behavior, but need to be. Chronicle the new things that seem to be on the horizon, but you have not yet incorporated into your life.

4. **What's confusing?** Write about those things that continue to be a source of question, wonderment, and even hurt. What are the things that you know need to be sorted out? What in your day or life needs resolution?

LEANING

I used to pray that I shall be saved from eternal death, but now I pray to be saved from shallow living.

—Macrina Wiederkehr, *Seasons of the Heart*

Most would agree that we should act on those things that God has spoken to us, or revealed as we have sought Him. But, most would also agree that we often don't actually press deeply into those new truths and revelations—that each of us are guilty of often just dipping our toes into the cool waters of these truths and insights, stopping far short of full immersion and total commitment.

Coaching (and mentoring) typically fall into the important, but not urgent basket for us as leaders. The value of kindred outside voices and help—especially when it means providing each of us some needed accountability—is rarely disputed, but even more rarely actively sought out.

Scripture is clear that we have been placed into community and the Body of Christ because we can not get "there" alone (1 Corinthians 12; Romans 12). And, in the same vein, we can't get to clarity alone. The multitude of one-another references have been woven throughout the New Testament for a reason.

Coaching and mentoring have become buzzwords in recent years and are now consistently talked about when one reads books and articles related to the core components of leadership today. One of the reasons that leaders seldom access both coaching and mentoring is due, in part, to some myths and misunderstanding concerning their purpose.

Coaching stands alongside and draws out what is already on the inside (Proverbs 20:5), whereas mentoring has gone before and places new resources and experience within. Most of what people view coaching to be is actually mentoring. And one of the biggest reasons why mentoring is not accessed more is because of what I like to call the "Yoda" syndrome: where we are left looking for the one, old, wise, and powerful sage with all of the answers, as opposed to seeing and accessing the potential of multiple mentors, including—but certainly not limited to—peer mentors.

Every Christ-follower needs a coach. Every coach needs a coach. The skill of asking good questions and helping each other draw up that which is within—that which the Spirit has already placed inside—is an essential skill for any leader in this day and age. Peer coaching, the idea of adopting the posture of coaching in order to help a peer process, is a valuable tool and complement to a more "formal" coaching relationship. Sometimes, Christ-followers and leaders need to invest in a structured relationship with a trained coach. But, Christ-followers consistently benefit from asking colleagues, good friends, and others around them for help in processing their thoughts, ideas, and questions.

Mentoring is tied to the exchange of resources. Obtaining mentors is typically tied first to reviewing where one wants or needs to go, and then determining some of the resources one will need to get there. There are more mentors around you than you know who can help you. But mentors prove to be the most help when they are able to match their skills and experiences with what you view to be your presenting "need."

Once again, peers are a source often overlooked when it comes to mentoring. These are those who are at a similar stage as yourself, who are seeking to address similar issues, or have similar needs. The benefits of peer mentoring come from hearing another's journey, gaining access to resources that you may not be aware of, and recognizing that you're not alone as many of the answers you seek are also the ones others are looking for.

There are also contemporary and historical mentors to help those who still find it difficult to find mentors, or are isolated because of geography or the loneliness that comes from pioneering. Biographies from the past, biblical figures from Scripture, and contemporary leaders who write and speak are all potential mentors for you if you alter your paradigm of mentoring.

The discipline of coaching and mentoring is really the intentional acknowledgement and practical focus to surround yourself with those who are committed to helping you think out loud in order draw out the insights God is sharing with you. It's an ongoing commitment as a leader to learn and grow from the insights of others (resourcing and helping to advance you ideation and character). Christ-followers who finish well are lifelong learners. Those who learn the most are those who value and invite the input, challenges, and questioning of others on a consistent basis.

HOW TO LEAN ON OTHERS

Here are four suggestions when it comes to adopting a posture of leaning on others and accessing the tremendous help that can come from coaching and mentoring.

First, assume personal responsibility for your own growth and development. All of us would love for someone to come up and offer all the help we need, but it's rare in our day for that to occur. You will have to take the first step. Look for those who you feel might be able to help. Be bold! Buy them a cup of coffee, ask to grab a few minutes after church, or find a time to meet. Whatever you do, ask!

Second, spend some time beforehand thinking through the kind of help you feel like you need. Doing so will help you to provide a concise summary of where you are, where you think God is leading you, and how you might need help. This will help a coach or mentor best assess whether or not he or she is in a position to help you.

Third, recognize that you need multiple coaches and mentors, not just that "one size fits all" person. One person simply cannot address all of the issues and factors you're facing. The more you can look to multiple coaches and mentors, the more the pressure is off those coaches or mentors to provide everything you need.

Fourth, identify your biblical mentor. Look at Scripture and identify the biblical character that most approximates your passion, calling, or desires. Study his or her life. Identify all the passages in Scripture that speak regarding their life and read them for life lessons, values, core behaviors, how God shaped their life, and what you can learn from their successes and failures.

THINKING IT OVER
You | One-to-One | Coaching | Group

Below is a guide to help you better process what you've just read. It can be used as you review the ideas personally, as a one-to-one discussion tool, as a small group interaction guide, or as a resource for a coaching conversation between you and a personal development coach.

If you are using *Awakening* with a small group, the following provides reflection questions for your sixth group conversation.

Reflect on the following quotes:

In Jesus we have a master to whom we do not sufficiently listen. He speaks to each heart the Word of life, the only word, but we do not listen.

—Jean-Pierre de Caussade, *The Sacrament of the Present Moment*

Prayer is a disciplined dedication to paying attention. Without single-minded attentiveness of prayer we will rarely hear anything worth repeating or catch as vision worth asking anyone else to gaze upon.

—John Westerhoff III and John Eusden, *The Spiritual Life*

Reflect on the following biblical text:

Psalm 19

Reflect on the following questions:

- **Listening**: What are they keys to being a "good listener" when it comes to your relationship with Christ? How do you personally know when you hear God speak?
- **Chronicling**: There are many forms and ways to journal/chronicle your thoughts as you process the Awakening Transition. What's your way? How can you do your way better? When/how often?

- **Leaning**: What helps you the best to lean in and discern what God is saying: using a coach to process out loud or using a coach to process conclusions you've already reached?

> **WANT MORE?**
>
> Here is a link to Leader Breakthru's Website that will take you further on topics covered in this chapter:
>
> **www.leaderbreakthru.com/spiritual-disciplines**

7

traps

CONDITIONED RESPONSES

If you want to identify me, ask me not where I live, or what I like to eat, or how I comb my hair, but ask me what I think I am living for, in detail, and ask me what I think is keeping me from living fully the thing I want to live for. Between these two answers you can determine the identity of any person. The better answer he has, the more of a person he is.

—THOMAS MERTON, *NO MAN IS AN ISLAND*

(Zack Curry)

RESPONSES

As Merton writes on the previous page, "Ask me what I think is keeping me from living fully the thing I want to live for." Am I living fully? What is holding me back? Both are critical questions for the person facing the Awakening Transition.

Conditioned responses are well-orchestrated traps we set for ourselves. They are reinforced by an enemy who is hoping to distract, sidetrack, derail, and even devour the potential response of a Christ-follower to the "awakening" call of God on his or her life. In the next few pages, we seek to highlight three of these conditioned responses that often flare up during the Awakening Transition.

Zack Curry is a leader who has walked through the Awakening Transition. Zack encountered many of the same experiences Kyle went through on the way to clarifying God's calling and direction for his life. Zack's focus in these next three sections is to identify three obstacles that Christ-followers often experience when encountering and seeking to respond to God's awakening call.

THE NEED TO COMPARE

It's an amazing thing to discover what you were created to do and to be able to gain new clarity on the unique contribution God has entrusted you with to make in the building of His Kingdom. Knowing your calling and leading out of a place of passion are desires and longings many people yearn for, especially young leaders. One of the key points from the Awakening Transition in my own journey was not only recognizing that I was in a transition and identifying my unique contribution, but also becoming aware of the things that had been hindering me.

I started leading at a pretty young age. In my sophomore year of high school, I was leading a student leadership team of about 10 people that oversaw a campus ministry that grew to over 200 students. We were a part of a passionate network of students in our city and region to see our schools encounter God and be transformed. We saw many saved, healed, and come alive with a contagious passion for Jesus. That impact carried forward into different churches as it spread to cities all over Northern California. For me, those days were a crash course in leadership that to this day I am so grateful for. Since then, I've been through multiple transitions, yet the Awakening Transition has been one of the most significant in the past few years.

Looking back over my journey, I've discovered that there have been a few common obstacles that I've faced from the time I was a young leader in high school to today. But it wasn't until I was in coaching sessions with Terry that I was able to finally clearly identify and define these different struggles. At various points in my journey, I would get so frustrated because I would be in a new season and out of nowhere the same challenges, insecurities, or points of conflict that I had faced before would seem to pop up out of nowhere. I would say to myself, "I thought I've already dealt with this!" or "Why am I going through this again?" The reality was that most of the time I had, but God was often taking me deeper into Him as a leader. God uses persistent struggles like these in each of our lives to cultivate new levels of maturity and spiritual authority. What was a breakthrough for me was that identifying and understanding these obstacles was not only a key for me as a leader in my own growth, but also for how I could better lead others. In fact, the more I began to process and share what I was learning, the more it freed me and others to be whom God had called us to be.

THE TEMPTATION OF COMPARISON

I believe one of the greatest hindrances to discovering our "unique" contributions in extending Christ's Kingdom is comparison. Whether you're waiting for a promise or in the middle of living it out, a huge temptation is to compare yourself with others and, in turn, lose focus on who God has created you to be. We're often unable to hear, see, or clearly move into who He has created us to be because we get caught in the trap of comparing who we are—or who we think we should be—with others. This has been a huge obstacle that I've had to overcome at different seasons of my own journey.

From a young age, I've had a passionate desire to be all that God has made me to be. I'm a visionary and dreamer with a hunger to see significant things happen. I long to be a part of a move of God that becomes a fire that sweeps in and transforms families, cities, culture, and nations. I long to see hearts awakened, people encountering the true God, and even see millions saved and the name of Jesus would be famous across the earth. Don't get me going! However, my zeal, passion, and genuine desire to be a part of something significant for the Kingdom of God has, at times, caused me to seek to bypass or even skip the process of what God has been at work doing in my own life by getting caught comparing myself to others, losing sight of who I am, and taking matters into my own hands. This behavior I can often exhibit is fueled by my need for approval, various insecurities related to my identity, and a flat-out lack of trust in the God who created me. I struggle, questioning whether what I am is enough. If you have any of these same battles, know you're not alone.

God refines leaders through opportunity. He often makes them wait. When a leader also has more opportunity than time, He makes them decide and become more focused. When a leader or Christ-follower has many has gifts, desires, and abilities all ready to be actualized and then the doors don't open, their need to trust can often go sideways and become a time when they try to force their way forward, hoping to prove they have what it takes, especially when compared to others are making things happen and are cutting things through.

Too often, I have jumped, seeking the approval of others and wanting other leaders or people around me to recognize, call out, validate, and acknowledge that I have what it takes to be a leader. The problem is simple: what I am seeking from others I should be getting first and foremost from God. On a long walk one day, battling my way through another moment like the one I just described, God led me to Psalm 57:2: "I cry out to God Most High, to God, who fulfills his purpose for me."

The words on the page jumped out at me and struck right to my heart. I was becoming impatient because things weren't lining up, doors weren't opening, and I wasn't being recognized. I was looking around at everyone else who seemed to have everything going their way. In God's kindness, He gently reminded me that He alone was the one who fulfills the purpose for my life and that I needed to stop comparing myself to others and put my trust in Him alone.

In high school, I constantly compared myself to my best friend. Our personalities were very different: I was relational and he was organized and structured. We took this leadership test once that identified your strengths and paired them with various biblical characters. His was Paul and mine was David. I was so upset with the results, convinced that I should've been Paul. No matter what strength, test, or accomplishment, I continually compared myself to him. What I did, who I was, and who God had made me to be was never enough. To be honest, it's pretty comical looking back, but at the time it was a huge struggle. What made it harder was I then began to try to be somebody that I really wasn't. It took other mature leaders around me to get perspective and tell me to just be who God had created me to be.

It was during some of my coaching conversations with Terry that God began to bring to the surface this pattern. When I'm in the midst of a transition, I increase my comparison with others even more. I also began to notice that the times I felt most alive and making my greatest impact were when I was contributing out of the strengths and purpose God had revealed to me. Comparing myself to others really was a counterfeit distraction that always took me away from making an authentic contribution to others.

COMPARE OR CULTIVATE

Comparison is clearly a strategy of the enemy to keep Christ-followers and leaders from being all that God has created them to be. The answer, however, is not just to stop comparing ourselves to other people. The answer is to understand the unique way we have each been shaped and called by God to contribute to others. Knowing who we are means also coming to terms with who we aren't. In order to fully embrace your strengths and develop into the leader and follower God has called you to be, you have to identify who you aren't and be okay with it. The point and reality is that your weakness is someone else's strength.

I grew up playing team sports like soccer, basketball, and baseball. I love being on a team and have learned so much about leadership and life through sports. One of the clear lessons is that a team needs a variety of strengths to win and be great. Take soccer, for example. You need a variety of skills and strengths to make a strong team. The defender, playmaker, scorer, keeper—the list goes on. Together, a good team blends multiple strengths and positions to work together to accomplish a common goal.

An orchestra is another helpful example of this. You need multiple instruments to make a beautiful and moving piece of music. But for something good to occur, each individual musician must accept and focus on better cultivating his or her part—the strength, role, and contribution each has been gifted to make. Being just like someone else makes for confusion and it creates deficiency in the group's overall contribution.

Once we shift from comparing ourselves to others to cultivating the gifts and strengths God has created us to bring, something new begins to happen. If we focus on what we're called to do, then the temptation to compare ourselves to others really doesn't make sense and becomes less appealing. Our time, energy, and focus need to go towards cultivating who it is God has made us to be, not comparing ourselves with others.

THE TEMPTATION TO COPY

Copying what other leaders have done or what seems to be currently working for others can also be a trap when it comes to responding to God's awakening call on our lives. This trap is a bit harder to identify and describe. When I say copy, I'm not talking about plagiarism or stealing people's ideas and taking credit for them as my own. No, we need to talk about something much more subtle and dangerous.

Copying can mean going along with the status quo, choosing to emulate others. It's about trying to be or do that which has brought success to others, as opposed to allowing God to birth what He has placed deep inside of you. It actually goes beyond what we do into who we really are and why we do certain things, revealing our values and motives. Maybe the best way to describe what I'm talking about is to share some struggles from my own life.

From the previous section, you now know that my desire for the approval of others—being accepted—is a big deal. I sometimes go after things just to prove that I'm like everyone else and a part of that which is being sought after. The danger is that at different points, this desire has taken me down roads that lead to living a life in front of others that is more like them and less like me. Where things get off course is when I know I'm beginning to abandon and neglect who God has created me to be and the calling he has placed on my life because I'm simply copying the people and the context in which I find myself—all to get results and prove that I belong.

A great example of this comes from the life of David. We all know that as a young leader, he goes out to fight Goliath. In 1 Samuel 17:38-39, right before David is about to go fight, Saul tries to give him his armor: "So Saul clothed David with his armor, and he put a bronze helmet on his head; he also clothed him with a coat of mail. David fastened his sword to his armor and tried to walk, for he had not tested them. And David said to Saul, 'I cannot walk with these, for I have not tested them.' So David took them off."

Did you catch what David says here? "I cannot walk with these, for I have not tested them." It was a great honor to be given the king's armor, but David knew it wouldn't work to take on another's identity. He would be putting on something that he himself had no experience with. The key to David's greatness was being David, whether others thought he belonged in that battle or not. His confidence could only be rooted in being who God had taught and shaped him to be, regardless of the context and its needs. That was the only way it could work. The story would have ended very differently if David went into battle with Saul's armor.

We have too many leaders today simply copying what they see in other leaders. There's a big difference between admiring, respecting others, and seeking to copy emulate their very characteristics. If we simply copy them because what they're doing has had success, we're neglecting the call of God on our own lives and that each of us have been fearfully and wonderfully made. As followers of Jesus, we have the single greatest message of hope and transformation to the world around us: our lives being changed. God is raising up authentic followers who are willing to display an authentic faith —not one in need of copying what others are doing. If we are created in the image of God, we have to believe that we carry the solution to some of the greatest needs, voids, and hopeless situations around us. Ephesians 2:10 says, "For we are His workmanship, created in Christ Jesus for good works, which God prepared beforehand that we should walk in them."

God has uniquely created us for good works. As leaders, this is pretty significant. Psalm 139:13-16 says this:

For You formed my inward parts;
You covered me in my mother's womb.
I will praise You, for I am fearfully and wonderfully made;
Marvelous are Your works,
And that my soul knows very well.
My frame was not hidden from You,
When I was made in secret,
And skillfully wrought in the lowest parts of the earth.
Your eyes saw my substance, being yet unformed.
And in Your book they all were written, the days fashioned for me
When as yet there were none of them.

I fear that much of our valuable time as leaders is wasted on copying what we know, instead of creating new answers for that which we don't know. If we're to genuinely reach our cities, see change in society, and transform culture, then we need a wide range of godly anointed leaders who don't all look the same. We need businessmen and women, actors, doctors, athletes, teachers, scientists, and pastors to all be filled with the Spirit of God, seeking Him for solutions and contending for life right where God has given them a platform and influence. I firmly believe that a significant component of the decay of the society around us is due to the fact that so much of the Christian community seeks to look like all the other parts, as opposed to birth new expressions of the faith.

My approval addiction has brought with it the temptation to copy what I know or see around me. As I've gradually begun to identify and accept who God has made me to be and as I've worked my way through this Awakening Transition, I've grown in my understanding of who it is that God has created me to be and I've accepted His challenge of clarifying what is it God has designed for me to create!

If you spend your days copying what works for others, then you won't have the time to invest in creating what God has destined for you to create. It's hard to do both and to do them as acts of authentic worship to our King. I say let's awaken to the call to be a part of creating something that takes time, expresses our unique identity, and shows us to be image-bearers of our creator God.

THE CHALLENGE TO COMPETE

The challenge to compare. The temptation to copy the success of others. And, finally, the feeding of our ambition by seeking to turn ministry into grounds for competition.

I'm really competitive, and I've been that way since I was a kid. In fact, I was so competitive as a young boy that I would be emotionally crushed whenever I lost a game. Thankfully, my parents saw this pattern that was developing in my life and began to work with me in this area. My mom would play board games or different sports and not let me win, as parents often do when their children are younger. In fact, she would try to find as many opportunities as she could for me to lose, so she could work with me in responding the right way. I didn't lose heart or my competitive edge, but I learned how to hold my composure and not fall apart. I can remember one year I was on a little league team that lost every game of the season. I got so frustrated and wanted to quit the team, but my dad wouldn't let me. He taught me about fighting for the team, never quitting, and finishing what you start.

Competition can take various forms in leadership and ministry. Sometimes it's not as obvious as others. Competition can also be healthy. As I mentioned earlier, I grew up playing team sports like soccer, basketball, and baseball. Some of these teams won championships, some were okay, and some where outright terrible. Through the years, I've seen different types of athletes and team dynamics. One thing that was an obvious principle in the success or failure of a team was how everyone on the team worked together.

If we're comparing ourselves with others or we're copying what others do in order to fit in and get noticed, we can almost without notice need to sustain ourselves by showing ourselves to be better than others and can begin to compete with those around us. Whether we realize it or not, our actions or motivations become driven by this.

Often, we don't even realize that this is what's driving us. I've often found myself in the midst of doing really good things but noticing that something was off inside of me! After stopping and taking a step back, often using my coach, friend, or wife to speak truth into me, I gain perspective that my root issue and motivation is often one of proving myself to be better. If what I'm doing, no matter how good it is, appears to be not getting the results I say I should be making, I often push the "I am better than them" button.

As Christ-followers and leaders, we are called to serve and empower others—which is how Christ chose to advance his Kingdom. True fruit is seeing others thrive and grow. If we're constantly competing with others around us, this becomes impossible to achieve. Not to mention unhealthy! Though few are willing to admit it, when we see a ministry or team like us succeed, it often can bring out a competitiveness that works directly opposite of Christ's upside-down Kingdom.

There are other ways competition creeps in. We often compete with the "ambition" or "pre-conceived visions" of what success looks like within ourselves. And if we aren't careful, those can wander right back into things that were started for right purposes, but become a threat to that which was good and right to do. A classic example of this is having to recreate a successful event, when God intended it to be a "one-off" experience. The end result is that we spend our time competing and recreating, instead of contributing around the calling God has entrusted to each of us and the community in which we are a part.

A quick story. I was a sophomore in high school on a mission trip to the Philippines. I was part of a team of about 15 people. About halfway through the trip, a few people on the team were really starting to get on my nerves. We were living in close quarters, eating together, traveling together, doing longs days of ministry—basically we did everything together. This meant that we all saw the best and worst of each other. I remember being at the end of my rope and spending some coveted time alone away from the group reading my Bible and journaling and being led to the verses below:

> Therefore, putting away lying, "Let each one of you speak truth with his neighbor," for we are members of one another. "Be angry, and do not sin": do not let the sun go down on your wrath, nor give place to the devil. Let him who stole steal no longer, but rather let him labor, working with his hands what is good, that he may have something to give him who has need. Let no corrupt word proceed out of your mouth, but what is good for necessary edification, that it may impart grace to the hearers. And do not grieve the Holy Spirit of God, by

whom you were sealed for the day of redemption. Let all bitterness, wrath, anger, clamor, and evil speaking be put away from you, with all malice. And be kind to one another, tenderhearted, forgiving one another, even as God in Christ forgave you (Ephesians 4:25-32, NKJV).

I was instantly convicted. Something in this passage jumped out at me: "Let him who stole steal no longer, but rather let him labor, working with his hands what is good, that he may have something to give him who has need."

The trap, then, is this: if we put our focus on the wrong thing, we put ourselves in danger of missing the real thing Jesus has called us to do or accomplish. In this verse, I initially thought that "Let him who stole steal no longer" was a reference to the enemy. Then I realized that the next part ruled him out. The enemy can't produce "something to give him who is in need." This verse is talking about us.

When we compete with others, I believe we are stealing from the world, our relationships, and those around us to whom God has called us to contribute. After all, James 4:1-3 describes the source of our fighting and struggle:

What causes fights and quarrels among you? Don't they come from your desires that battle within you? You desire but do not have, so you kill. You covet but you cannot get what you want, so you quarrel and fight. You do not have because you do not ask God. When you ask, you do not receive, because you ask with wrong motives, that you may spend what you get on your pleasures.

If we're asking for the good of those around us and our motives aren't for our own fame but to see the goodness of God released to a dying world, everything changes. We're no longer competing, but joining God in what He has done from the beginning of time: giving to bring life, hope, and transformation. Of course, I haven't yet completely mastered the temptation to compare, copy, or compete. However, I know what it looks like, so I pay closer attention to what is motivating me and I fiercely guard what it is that God has called me to cultivate, create, and contribute to the places where He has given me influence.

In the end, what will you choose? I challenge you to cultivate instead of compare, create instead of copy, and contribute instead of compete.

THINKING IT OVER
You | One-to-One | Coaching | Group

Below is a guide to help you better process what you've just read. It can be used as you review the ideas personally, as a one-to-one discussion tool, as a small group interaction guide, or as a resource for a coaching conversation between you and a personal development coach.

If you are using *Awakening* with a small group, the following provides reflection questions for your seventh group conversation.

Reflect on the following quote:

> *The real question is, "What does this have to say to me?" Those who are totally converted comes to every experience and ask not whether or not they like it, but what does it have to teach them. "What's the message in this for me? What's the gift in this for me? How is God in this event? Where is God in this suffering?"*
>
> —Richard Rohr, *Everything Belongs*

Reflect on the following biblical text:

Psalm 13

Reflect on the following questions:

- Which of the three patterns (compare, copy, and compete) might cause you to miss what God is saying and doing in your journey? Which do you sense could be occurring during this transition?
- What or who do you compare yourself to? Why?
- What or who do you find yourself copying? Why?
- What or who do you try to beat? Why?
- If there's one fear you're facing related to moving into or beyond the Awakening Transition, what might that be?

awakening

WANT MORE?

Here is a link to Leader Breakthru's Website that will take you further on topics covered in this chapter:

www.leaderbreakthru.com/leading-with-spiritual-authority

8
forwarding

*The main place you do the work of God is as you go along.
It doesn't have to be in the high-profile or important positions.
It will happen, if it happens at all, in the routine, unspectacular
corners of life. As you go along.*

—JOHN ORTBERG, *LOVE BEYOND REASON*

RSVP

All formal invitations come with a mechanism that helps to facilitate a response from the recipient known to most as a RSVP. The term RSVP comes from the French expression "répondez s'il vous plait," which means simply, "please respond."

The sender of an invitation requests your attendance and participation in a future event, and wants to know your intentions. General invitations are sometimes send to a more generic audience, going out to the many with an assumption that many—but not all—will actually attend. But when the RSVP appears, it indicates that a specific individual or party has been "specifically invited" and that a place has been personally reserved in light of his or her possible attendance. To complete and finalize that potential, the invitation must be accepted through a formal response.

The Awakening Transition brings with it an "invitation." It's the same one Jesus extended to both the early disciples and to people like Kyle. Like them, we too are given the invitation to begin the journey to address the deepest longing found in each of our hearts. It is another "one of many options" to be considered. This is "the" invitation to experience life to its fullest, to participate in the abundant life we hear about in passages of Scripture like John 10. It's the call to awaken one's soul to life and purpose as God intends. The long-awaited King came bringing to earth the Kingdom of God. He came not to negotiate the choice, but rather to offer the terms of surrender in order to experience this new life. In order for life to occur and for the Kingdom to come, one needed to accept the terms of the King.

I'll never forget when I heard the Gospel presented in the context of the Kingdom of God. I was sitting under the teaching of a now good friend, Jan Hettinga, and listening to him share his insights from his book, *Follow Me*. The thrust of his teaching couched the salvation message beyond the "ticket to heaven." Christ came to offer forgiveness for our sin through his sacrifice on the cross, and by announcing that "the kingdom of heaven has come near" (Matthew 3:2). Finally, the pieces of the puzzle began to fit together. Our King, who made the choice before time began to offer His life as ransom for my sin, was not offering an invitation to play our part in the extension of His Kingdom to others. Christ's call was for men and women like each of us—who are full of anger, hatred, and self-defended barriers—to lay down our arms and surrender to His rule and reign as the only true leader. It was the Kingdom offered through His mercy and grace that was founded upon Christ's death and resurrection from the cross, offering the one and final answer to the rebellion and insurrection that has occurred over the course of human history. Jesus came offering to us—and those like us—the only terms that could be offered for ending the battle of sin that has been fought since the beginning of humanity's existence. To adopt a developmental paradigm, it's a call and an invitation to align with God's work on our behalf. And it is the beginning of a journey of discovery.

Jesus is building His Church. He is the cornerstone of that Church. His plans are for more than just the life beyond. It is for His Kingdom to come and His will to be done. His invitation is for us to join Him in this endeavor. He has a place for each of us in this adventure. It is in understanding that narrative and seeing our lives fitting into that much larger story that our lives have meaning and purpose. It is a new life to which we are called. God's redemption of humanity, the ushering in of the Kingdom of God, is what is now being played out in space and time. And we are invited to participate.

In the United States, we have a generation of people who say they believe in Christ, but refuse to follow him as King. Life in Christ has been promoted and sold as an attractive offer or "option" to help each us obtain eternal life. Across our country, churches are filled with attenders who come each week to consume goods and receive benefits. As consumers, many then pick and choose the truth that most appeals to their current "needs," often with very little thought of repentance or surrender and submission to Christ.

Christians are often recognized by those outside of the Church as a "right" wing political movement, as opposed to a radical move of God offering His Kingdom to end the insurrection of humanity. The Awakening Transition seeks to signal to those who hunger and long for true life the chance to realign one's life direction and behavior around a life of truth and real hope. It's a calling to live for so much more—as opposed to settle for so much less.

I speak at various men's retreats throughout any given year. We use this kind of language of the Gospel at our retreats. We've adopted the imagery of a battle at hand, with the call for men to stand up and join a "Band of Brothers" that fight for the hearts of men and women, as well as for Christ's church. We call men to arms. And they respond. But it's also been interesting that when they come home, it's more than just a mountaintop experience, as the women of these men tell of also wanting into that same battle. God has birthed into the hearts of men and women alike a longing for Him and for a life that makes a difference. It's a call to live life and to take up the swords and shields of faith in order to align with a greater purpose—the Kingdom cause.

I realize that this battle imagery doesn't appeal to everyone. Many have had to participate in the ravages of war, and history tells of crusades and other violent evils done under the flags of the Church. With all that said, though, I'm still amazed at what happens when the people of God are challenged to participate in something bigger than themselves and the advance of Christ's Kingdom. They rise to the challenge to accept this invitation, and they embrace the call of God on their lives. These are the awakening moments that have stirred souls to that defining act of surrender and commitment to fight the good fight.

In the Awakening Transition, these are questions that Kyle and all Christ-followers must address. It's not about vocation; it's about all of life. God uses vocation to express the influence He has on each of our lives. It's the call to step out of the boat and into the raging seas of life, with eyes fixed on Jesus instead of the illusion that life can be "controlled." My guess is that God has already or is currently in the process of inviting you to respond. It's a lifelong calling, as opposed to just a trip to the altar. It's more than an option that will join many other options for your life. His is an invitation to choose a different kind of life.

This invitation includes a call for an RSVP. What's your response?

FORWARDING

Life beyond the Awakening Transition will consist of a series of assignments, tasks, choices, and the increased desire for spiritual growth and hearing the voice of God. Each will make key deposits of influence, playing its role in revealing who Christ has shaped you to be and what God is shaping you to do. Choices will present themselves to check our alignment with Christ's work. Integrity checks, value clarification, faith challenges, and authority insights will present themselves in the days ahead. As you move forward, greater clarity will come to your personal calling. Our callings are dynamic. The more we live into them, the clearer they become.

Great questions challenge us to go to new places in our understanding and behavior. The questions a Christ-follower asks can help facilitate his or her ongoing development. The more strategic the question, the greater the discovery. Good coaching is about good questions. As we develop, the questions change. It's possible—likely, even—that the questions you'll be asking 10 years from now will be different ones than you're asking right now. Because of this, identifying the right questions is often of first importance when one seeks the right answers.

At its core, personal calling seeks to respond to three core questions. Each is simple, yet together they are strategic and offer direction and focus to Christ-followers:

1. **Perspective**: Where have you been?
   Based now on seeing the past from God's perspective...

2. **Direction**: Where are you going?
   Based now on seeing the future from God's perspective...

3. **Identity**: Whom has God provided to help you take the next steps?

These three core questions help Christ-followers set their compasses to true north. They help provide needed clarity, focus, and direction, propelling an individual toward greater fruitfulness in terms of Kingdom contribution. Answering these three questions will help unlock the essential components of personal calling. Perspective, direction, identity.

A personal calling statement is an individual's—and this is key!—best-understanding-to-date of where they are in the process of understanding God's leading in his or her life. Contrary to what we are often led to believe, statements like these are not once-and-for-all declarations. Instead, they serve their most important purpose as a directional guide, similar to our latest "GPS" reading. The more each of us aligns with what God is at work doing, the clearer one's call and guidance becomes.

A personal calling statement is also not a statement of vain wishes, ambition, or self-made dreams to somehow win over God's favor. Instead, this statement is a summation of one's discovery of God's intent. Good calling statements can be translated into day-to-day action, as well as long-term future behavior. They are concise and easy to be referenced. They are not to be tucked away in a notebook. They are the first pages, a guide as we seek to live out our life visions. Let's look more closely at each of the three questions related to personal calling.

WHERE HAVE YOU BEEN?

In his book *A Resilient Life,* Gordon MacDonald candidly shares reflections back on the early days of his development:

> "In my early 30s, I was too blessed with seeming boundless energy, with a self-confidence bordering on hubris, and a practical conviction that thinking quickly on your feet can get you just about anywhere. 'Today' was the important hour; tomorrow could take care of itself. What I was blind to was the fact that every 'yesterday' was informing the 'todays' of my life, and that every 'today' was formulating consequences that would become influential for the 'tomorrows.' They—the yesterdays, todays, and tomorrows—were all networked and interfacing with one another. They could not become compartmentalized."

If God has ever been at work in a Christ-follower's life, then He has always been at work. Like a plant, every future is seeded in the past. Therefore, looking back becomes the precursor to living forward. The most prolific command given to the nation of Israel was the call to remember. Resident in all of the feasts, festivals, and building of altars by the nation of Israel was to remember the past works of their God. The same challenge extends to each of us today and is the foundation of uncovering one's calling.

In the Focused Living Process we (Leader Breakthru) have seen literally thousands of individuals be able to look back at their past in order to better clarify their personal calling and future direction. The process has been intentionally designed to assist a Christ-follower gain sovereign perspective on his or her journey. The process involves mapping out God's shaping work to date (the creation of a personal timeline) and summarizing the past into a series of lessons and deposits that God has entrusted to a Christ-follower's care. It then involves writing a calling statement (the creation of a personal calling statement) and the identification of the resources needed to accomplish one's calling (the creation of a personal mentoring constellation).

WHERE ARE YOU GOING?

Destination needs to be expressed on two fronts. First is the call to grow deeper in one's personal intimacy and dependency on Christ. Calling must be sourced in something greater than personal intent. It is sourced out of the deep reservoir of one's heart that continues to be renewed by living water, not yesterday's devotions. Where one is going is first addressed by identifying who is the source of one's future. Where one goes in his or her relationship with Christ serves to predetermine where a Christ-follower is able to go for Christ.

Second is the call to action. The call to do, undergirded by the call to be, now has mission beyond one's preferences. Personal vision is a word-picture and stating of a future reality from God's perspective. It serves to help propel a Christ-follower from where they have been to a future state and good deeds that God has prepared for each Christ-follower to undertake.

It's important to note—especially for those in vocational ministry—that it's vital to separate personal vision from corporate vision. When the two become enmeshed, seeds of dysfunction can become planted. Those who lead organizations will have similar threads found in both their personal vision and that of the organization, but the more one is able to differentiate from the organization, the less the one becomes entangled or needs to make the organization succeed in order to validate one's worth.

Where do you think God is calling you? Where is your relationship with Him today? In what ways is God challenging you to go deeper with Him? When is it that you run and feel God's pleasure? What has God put on your heart that needs to come into existence?

The Focused Living Process helps a Christ-follower address this second question with a series of exercises related to clarifying his or her first order call (being/purpose) and an exercise that seeks to discover the next chapter of God's call (doing/vision). Purpose comes as he or she describes his or her identity in light of God's Word. Vision is the result of seeing the next chapters of one's development in light of the best understanding of the past and your former development.

WHO CAN HELP YOU GET THERE?

You don't get to clarity alone. It's just that simple. Mentors serve to deposit much-needed insights, resources, and experience, as well as serve to develop one's capacity to better recognize God's voice and desires. The community of believers that surrounds those seeking clarity provide peer mentoring and important forms of accountability and resourcing as they counsel our future growth and development. Multiple mentors allow for greater diversity in needs. There are at least nine types of mentors and three kinds of mentoring that can provide needed resources and assist in a leader's development and growth. The creation of a mentoring constellation and the development of a 100-day action plan help to translate new insights into behavioral change in critical seasons of implementation.

Discovering one's life purpose and calling brings greater focus to your life, increased effectiveness, and better decision-making in the future. As a Christ-follower increases in his or her clarity, issues switch from what one "could do" to that which God has uniquely gifted them to do and "should do." The many good things often must give way to the fewer, best things. Often, it's not a matter of good and bad, but better and best.

FOCUSED LIVING: PERSONAL CALLING RETREAT AND ONLINE PROCESS

Focused Living is a personal development process to help Christ-followers better clarify life direction and calling. Whether in the live, retreat format or through the online process, Focused Living walks you step-by-step through the creation of a personal calling statement.

Leader Breakthru offers two additional personal development processes and personal development coaching to help you take your Focused Living insights deeper in order to gain greater traction in your life. Coaching helps leaders move from breakthrough insights to new behavior.

To learn more about Focused Living, visit our website: www.leaderbreakthru.com/focused-living

UP AHEAD

The first days are essential to any important decision time of a Christ-follower. Choosing to follow Christ early on in one's development is an act of submission and surrender. It involves awakening to the call of Christ. In each generation, God's people are given the opportunity to respond to this invitation and call. It is a calling to be a distinct people used by God to demonstrate and proclaim hope. In each generation, God awakens the hearts of His followers to the unique and personal call He has placed on their lives. It's a call as common to the early days of relationship with humanity, yet as young as the fresh surrender during the Awakening Transition of a Christ-follower. What will be your response? What part will you play in being part of the answer? May your heart awaken to God's unique and personal call for you.

Up ahead, as you continue to clarify and live out your calling, you'll experience the need for more. Up ahead, a hunger will begin to rise to the surface to move on from calling to identifying one's unique contribution. Up ahead, you'll encounter the second of three strategic transitions—the Deciding Transition. Up ahead, you'll experience challenges beyond life direction. As calling is lived out, there comes a time when leaders must prioritize their focus and begin to say "no" to the good options, so that they are better equipped to say "yes" to a unique contribution.

The second book in this series is entitled *Deciding* and it's focus is helping unpack the second major transition, which we've called the Deciding Transition. Additionally, the APEX Personal Development Process from Leader Breakthru brings greater clarity to a Christ-follower's unique, personal contribution. This process helps individuals discover issues related to their major role and effective methods, and provides a decision-making grid called a "Personal Life Mandate" that will help to guide the choices that lay ahead.

THINKING IT OVER

You | One-to-One | Coaching | Group

Below is a guide to help you better process what you've just read. It can be used as you review the ideas personally, as a one-to-one discussion tool, as a small group interaction guide, or as a resource for a coaching conversation between you and a personal development coach.

If you are using *Awakening* with a small group, the following provides reflection questions for your eighth group conversation.

Reflect on the following quote:

It was as though some gave me permission to be me, and do what I most wanted to do. "I felt something deep in side of me relax" I later wrote in my journal, "and say yes." There was no audible voice, nothing dramatic save the starry sky, but some deep part of me knew what I was to be about.

—Timothy Jones, *Awake My Soul*

Reflect on the following biblical text:

Psalm 23

Reflect on the following questions:

- What's your RSVP to the invitation of Christ?
- If you have yet to respond, what does it mean now to you?
- If you've responded before, how does reading about the Awakening Transition help you think about things differently?
- If God were to have His way in terms of where He might lead you in the future, or what He might ask you to do, what do you think some next steps might be?

WANT MORE?

Here is a link to Leader Breakthru's Website that will take you further on topics covered in this chapter:

www.leaderbreakthru.com/focused-living-online

Appendix A: Small Group Guide

MEETING 1

Before the meeting, review the guide found on page 27. Have group members introduce themselves and then talk about their expectations for the meetings together. Open with prayer, praying back some of those expectations. Read the quote and talk about surrendering the direction of our lives back to Christ. Review Psalm 62 as group. Read chapter 1 together. Use the reflection questions to discuss the chapter. Ask group members to share their journeys to date. Discuss and interact with what each person shares. Close with prayer, asking the Holy Spirit to use the group meetings to lead and guide each person, as well as to provide the clarity he or she is seeking. (Note: Remind the group to read chapter 2 before the next meeting.)

MEETING 2

Before the meeting, review the guide found on page 42. Make sure your preparation includes time on the issue of Direction found in the Back Story section. Lead the group through a verse-by-verse praying of Psalm 86. Review the reflection questions. Also, go back and review together the Back Story section of chapter 2 to ensure that group members have a good understanding of calling as defined by *Awakening*. This meeting helps to establish that every Christian is called by God. (Note: Remind the group to read chapter 3 before the next meeting.)

MEETING 3

Before the meeting, review the guide found on page 56. Make sure your preparation includes time on the issue of direction found in the Back Story section. This chapter helps offer a foundational understanding of how God shapes a person over a lifetime, as well as the need to grow in our self-

Appendix A

awareness related to our identity in Christ. Review chapter 3 and read together Psalm 20. Discuss with group participants their view of the Awakening Transition, and what this insight means for their current situation. (Note: Remind the group to read chapter 4 before the next meeting.)

MEETING 4

Before the meeting, review the guide found on page 71. Read the quote from Wendell Berry to begin this session. God has always been at work shaping our lives. Remember the deeds of the Lord. Talk about your own story and your sense that God has been orchestrating your calling. Review chapter 4, as well as the reflection questions. Review where each person sees himself or herself in regards to the Transition Life Cycle. Close the session with prayer, asking God for clarity in direction and future direction. (Note: Remind the group to read chapter 5 before the next meeting.)

MEETING 5

Before the meeting, review the guide found on page 90. This meeting discusses the Awakening Transition coming to an end—the Direction Phase of a transition. First, review Kyle's story and the new direction he received. What stood out to each of the group members about the end of a transition? What could God be doing both in areas of character (being) and competency (skills) in the group members? Review the Tournier quote and Psalm 25. Close the meeting by reviewing the *Awakening* Summary. (Note: Remind the group to read chapter 6 before the next meeting.)

MEETING 6

Before the meeting, review the guide found on page 102. This meeting seeks to discuss postures that help Christ-followers gain all they can out of their transition. Review this chapter together as a group. Talk about the ideas that seem most helpful. Which of the three postures have worked in the past for the group members? Which might they want to explore as a result of this transition? Open up discussion for group members to be able to share what they continue to experience, as well as what they need from God as they work through their transition. (Note: Remind the group to read chapter 7 before the next meeting.)

MEETING 7

Before the meeting, review the guide found on page 117. This meeting goes after ways individuals often avoid the work that God intends to accomplish through the Awakening Transition. Even well-meaning believers resort to comparing, copying, or competing instead of going deeper with God, and allowing Him to forge a new work in our lives. Review each pattern. Talk about what the group members have observed. To which would they be most susceptible? Finish this meeting with Psalm 13 and what it means to "trust in the Lord's unfailing love." (Note: Remind the group to read chapter 8 before the next meeting.)

MEETING 8

Before the meeting, review the guide found on page 128. This meeting seeks to bring closure to the discussions related to the Awakening Transition. This does not mean those in this transition are finished. The core idea of this meeting is challenging those within the group to respond to Christ's invitation and call. We close with a review of the familiar Psalm 23. Read this psalm with the Awakening Transition in mind. Close the time with prayer for each person and his or her ability to respond to God's shaping work.

Appendix B: Coaching Guide

This guide provides a generic example for utilizing *Awakening* in a series of coaching conversations. This coaching guide has been specifically developed for coaches who are coaching the personal development of Christian leaders, and seeking to help individuals clarify issues of life direction and calling. The prime candidates for this book and coaching guide are Christ-followers and leaders who are in their mid 20s to late 30s. The typical coaching structure is six coaching appointments (twice monthly for three months), each lasting approximately 45-60 minutes.

FIRST COACHING SESSION

Goal: Give an overview of the characteristics of a transition (see *Stuck!*, pages 8-10), the Awakening Transition, and clarify the desired outcome for this series of coaching appointments.

In this first appointment, the coach should start by laying a foundation related to the Awakening Transition.

Issues often addressed in this session include:

- Characteristics of a transition
- God does some of His most important work during times of transition
- Transitions are the in-between times, moving a Christ-follower to the next chapter

Key questions for this session include:

- Where have you been in your development?
- What do you think might be ahead?
- How do you think God might be at work during this time?

- How can I best help you? What do you hope to get from our time together?

Assignment: Read *Awakening*, chapters 1-2 and journal your thoughts.

SECOND COACHING SESSION

Goal: Gaining greater understanding of what led to this transition and defining some of the core characteristics of the Awakening Transition the individual is experiencing.

In this second appointment, the coach should explore the coachee's journey thus far—specifically, what issues contribute to the launch (Entry Phase) of the actual transition and what are the personal development issues that God could be developing or shaping.

Issues often addressed in this session include:

- Understanding the Transition Life Cycle (page 11)
- Understanding the definition of calling and what God seeks to clarify (chapter 1)
- Entering the transition and connection points with Kyle's story (chapter 2)

Key questions for this session include:

- What issues stood out to you as you read chapters 1-2 of the book?
- What clarity did you get regarding being in the Awakening Transition?
- What are some of your worries about this time? Your hopes? Your fears?
- What were some of the processing items God used to move you into the transition (e.g., isolation, conflict, difficulties, confusion, lack of results, etc.)?
- What are some of the issues God seems to be bringing to the surface?

Assignment: Read *Awakening*, chapter 3 and journal your thoughts.

THIRD COACHING SESSION

Goal: Identifying some of the core issues God is bringing to the surface within the individual, as well as exploring some of the core questions the individual has related to the past, the future, struggles with being in the in-between, impending decisions that lie ahead, etc.

In this third appointment, we are moving into the heart of God's processing and shaping work. Your role is not to solve, but surface the issues and questions.

Issues often addressed in this session include:

- Character processing
- Response patterns in the past when they have faced these issues
- What God might be calling for in terms of surrender, reconciliation, and alignment

Key questions for this session include:

- What did you learn about evaluation and alignment as you read chapter 3?
- What are some of the things God seems to be working on in you related to your character?
- What are some of the things God seems to be saying about you and how He wants to use you in the future?
- What are some of the obstacles to God using you in greater ways in the future?
- What's driving the impatience? Why are you in a hurry to get past this?

<u>Assignment</u>: Read the section titled, The Back Story: Identity on page 48 of *Awakening* and journal your thoughts.

FOURTH COACHING SESSION

Goal: Exploring obstacles to moving forward and how God is using this time to shape values and bring clarity to identity. (Reminder: As coach, the transition may continue far past your series of coaching sessions. Your role isn't to resolve the transition, but to help process the transition.)

In this fourth appointment, it's important to continue to listen to what God is doing, and help the individual identify what God is clarifying about who the individual is, as well as what God desires related to his or her identity into the future.

Issues often addressed in this session include:

- Core values
- Issues related to "being" and intimacy with God
- Issues related to greater self-awareness and becoming self-defined

Key questions for this session include:

- What did you learn about the evaluation-alignment phase as you read chapter 3?
- What are some of the things God seems to be working on related to your character?
- What are some of the things God seems to be saying about you and how he wants to use you in the future?
- What are some of the obstacles to God using you in greater ways in the future
- What's driving the impatience? Why are you in a hurry to get past this?

<u>Assignment</u>: Read *Awakening*, chapters 4-5 and journal your thoughts.

FIFTH COACHING SESSION

Goal: This session can be two-fold in terms of focus: (1) if the individual's transition is beginning to approach the end, use the thoughts below or (2) if his or her transition continues, begin to preview what the end will eventually look like using the thoughts below.

In this fifth appointment, we explore how God begins to reveal direction, as well as that the end takes time, often involving a series of steps. Because of this, it's important to continue to be patient and let God unfold His plan.

Issues often addressed in this session include:

- That destiny experiences are signals that answers are coming
- Allowing God to unfold future options vs. forcing the way forward
- That the end of a transition involves God challenging the individual's faith and trust.

Key questions for this session include:

- What stood out to you as you read about direction and a time of faith challenge?
- What have you begun to see/experience related to direction and ways forward?
- What might cause you to take things into your own hands?
- Talk about God's provision. What doubts (if any) does all of this bring to the surface?
- How could the enemy attack you right now?

<u>**Assignment**</u>: Read *Awakening*, chapters 6-7 and journal your thoughts.

SIXTH COACHING SESSION

Goal: This final session might be (1) time to help continue to process the transition and what has been learned, and/or (2) processing the end of the transition and launching into the next chapter of the individual's development.

In this sixth appointment, it's important to review the postures and traps, as well as solidify the gains related to the transition time and the coaching. In this final time, it's good for the coach and coachee to walk through chapter 8 as part of the call.

Issues often addressed in this session include:

- What are the ways they can continue to process God's shaping work?
- What could be the traps they might fall into after the coaching?
- Where to go from here?

Key questions for this session include:

- In what way did the chapter on postures help identify ways to continue to process your transition?
- With which of the three traps do you most identify? How will you not fall prey to these?
- What clarity have you gained related to who you are?
- What clarity have you gained related to your direction and calling?
- What choices are ahead of you to make sure you stay on track?

<u>Assignment</u>: Review – Focused Living Online Process (www.leaderbreakthru.com/focused-living-online)

the leadership development series

Leader Breakthru's Leadership Development Series consists of three books that take a closer look at the three significant transition moments that every Christ-follower will face. Each of these books can be used as a personal read, a small group resource or as a one-on-one coaching resource. For an introduction to the concept of transitions and an overview of these transitions, check out the book *Stuck! Navigating Life & Leadership Transitions,* by Terry Walling.

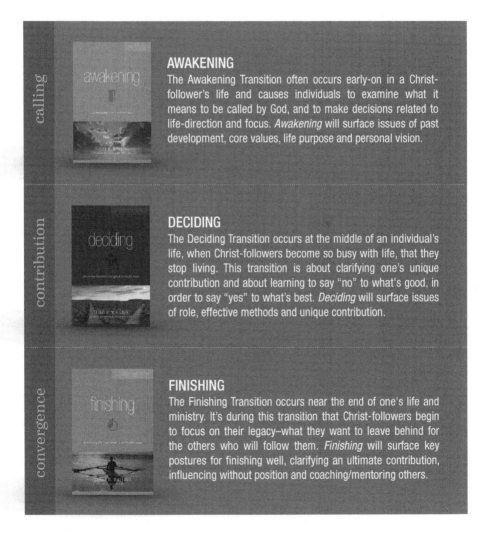

AWAKENING
The Awakening Transition often occurs early-on in a Christ-follower's life and causes individuals to examine what it means to be called by God, and to make decisions related to life-direction and focus. *Awakening* will surface issues of past development, core values, life purpose and personal vision.

DECIDING
The Deciding Transition occurs at the middle of an individual's life, when Christ-followers become so busy with life, that they stop living. This transition is about clarifying one's unique contribution and about learning to say "no" to what's good, in order to say "yes" to what's best. *Deciding* will surface issues of role, effective methods and unique contribution.

FINISHING
The Finishing Transition occurs near the end of one's life and ministry. It's during this transition that Christ-followers begin to focus on their legacy—what they want to leave behind for the others who will follow them. *Finishing* will surface key postures for finishing well, clarifying an ultimate contribution, influencing without position and coaching/mentoring others.

3 Core Processes™

Leader Breakthru offers three core, personal development processes that are designed to guide the on-going development of a Christ-follower. Together they comprise a leadership development system for churches, missions, ministries and organizations.

If you'd like more information about these processes, would like to go through one of the processes online, or would like to gain a license to facilitate one of the processes in your context, please visit: leaderbreakthru.com

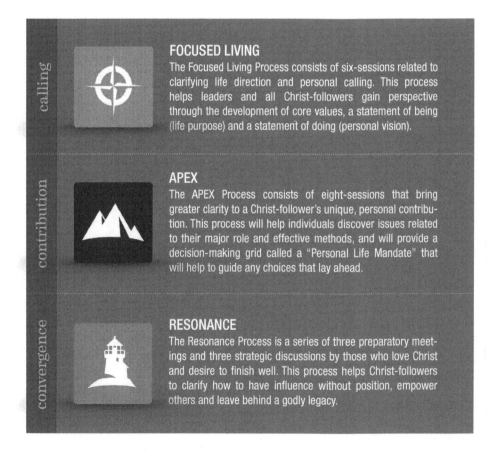

FOCUSED LIVING
The Focused Living Process consists of six-sessions related to clarifying life direction and personal calling. This process helps leaders and all Christ-followers gain perspective through the development of core values, a statement of being (life purpose) and a statement of doing (personal vision).

APEX
The APEX Process consists of eight-sessions that bring greater clarity to a Christ-follower's unique, personal contribution. This process will help individuals discover issues related to their major role and effective methods, and will provide a decision-making grid called a "Personal Life Mandate" that will help to guide any choices that lay ahead.

RESONANCE
The Resonance Process is a series of three preparatory meetings and three strategic discussions by those who love Christ and desire to finish well. This process helps Christ-followers to clarify how to have influence without position, empower others and leave behind a godly legacy.